June Crosby's

*An insider's guide
to San Diego area restaurants*

With over 70 selected recipes

CROSSTOWN PUBLICATIONS, INC.
La Jolla, California

ABOUT THE AUTHOR

Attractive, vivacious June Crosby is most widely known as the wife of famous band leader Bob Crosby and the mother of their five grown children. During her marriage she has probably traveled and cooked more than most women do. Bob and his Bobcats have been booked worldwide, so together June and Bob have toured Europe and the Orient, and even lived in Australia during which time June wrote for the Australian *Women's Weekly*. On the road she collects recipes from friends and special restaurants, and when home, wherever home is, she tests them out on her husband and guests.

From the beginning of their marriage, June kept a diary of recipes, people and places; and when she and Bob moved to Hawaii these culinary acquisitions were put to good use in her columns for the Honolulu *Star-Bulletin*. Returning to the mainland she continued writing for the San Diego *Union*, Elgin *Daily Courier-News*, Illinois *State Journal* and Sacramento *Union*.

Her next ventures led to magazines and books. In 1968 an article in *Woman's Day* was the forerunner of her book *Serve It Cold!*, co-authored by Ruth Conrad Bateman, and published by Doubleday and Co., Inc. in May of 1969. Later that fall June authored *Holiday Recipes,* published simultaneously by Home Federal Savings of San Diego and Pioneer Savings of Honolulu.

A frequent contributor to *Carte Blanche* and *Western's World* magazines, she is a member of Theta Sigma Phi and the National League of Penwomen. Spare time is devoted to the Mental Health Association of San Diego County, of which June and Bob have been Honorary Chairmen for the past three years. Last year they were honored with lifetime memberships.

Born in Chicago, the daughter of a renowned surgeon, she studied Pre-Med at Sarah Lawrence College and later at University of California at Los Angeles. Her intentions were to pursue psychiatry or pathology. Marriage and children altered this goal, but not entirely. Working with the Mental Health Association has given her much satisfaction and a sense of achievement. And Bob says, "June's kitchen is her 'lab,' in it she's continuously testing some new dish. It makes her happy, and me too. I eat all her mistakes . . . even *they* are delicious!"

ACKNOWLEDGMENTS AND CREDITS

The author wishes to thank the restaurateurs of San Diego and Baja California for their kindness in permitting their exclusive recipes to appear on these pages. It is hoped that this book will entice visitors and residents alike to dine in participating restaurants. To the "industry," my sincere appreciation...without their assistance there would have been no book.

To Louise Gault, my editor, who deals so well with words, without her expertise and encouragement I would have been lost. To Maxine Judkins, who did the leg-work coordinating the restaurant owners and chefs with my needs for their facts and recipes. To Susie Smith, who typed and retyped for hours and hours to produce perfect copy for the printers.

Thanks too, to Bo-Danica's Gifts, Lubach's Restaurant, Jurgensen's—La Jolla Store, Sleeper's Produce and the San Diego Fish Company for our select serving pieces and delectable ingredients. Their assistance helped Marie Kelley, the food stylist who followed my recipes, and photographer Charles Schneider, who snapped the scene of San Diego's skyline, create a both beautiful and bountiful cover. To Bob Perine, the art director at Frye & Smith, for "putting it all together." Unanimously, we ap-pre-c-iate.

Several of the recipes in this book first appeared in
Western's World Magazine, © 1970 by Frank M.
Hiteshew & Assoc. for Western Airlines International

Library of Congress Catalog Card Number 79-186129

INTRODUCTION

If there's one thing I've learned in thirty years of nomadic married life, it's a keen appreciation of good food! We've traveled throughout America, and in Asia, Australia, Canada, the Caribbean, Europe and Mexico, and we've eaten in all sorts of places from simple diners-on-the-road to restaurants of international gastronomical acclaim. As long as travel is part of our business, you can be sure "Where to eat?" will have a lion's share of our contemplation . . . for this is a particular pleasure my husband and I enjoy.

Friends here and there have guided us to delightful dinners, often in unpredictable places. We have beamed over unpretentious fine food at under $5.00 per person and had reason to bristle at some flops at $10.00 and up. We don't judge a restaurant's worth by the price of it's meals . . . in fact, sometimes a high meal check is just a camouflage for poor food and shameful service.

At each restaurant, Bob and I have sampled various dishes and eyed the service. We have not made our purpose known, nor have we accepted anything "on the house." At all times we tried to remain objective. It's so easy in your own home town to become mesmerized with a restaurant. It becomes "your place." For you that's where the action is; the service, food and people preclude your chancing a change, and you seldom venture into other worthy establishments. "Lost Horizons?" . . . variety *is* spice, but you'll never know comparable environments and menus if your very security inhibits an occasional adventure.

For the traveler it's something else. His restaurant pickings are made by guess and by golly, often solely de-

5

pendent on recommendations of hotel personnel or a taxi cab driver. In a nutshell I hope both to tempt San Diegans to visit a variety of restaurants, and offer visitors to this southwesternmost area of the U.S.A. an insider's guide to the best that's here.

It has been virtually impossible to canvas all of the San Diego County and Mexican border restaurants. If Bob and I have missed your favorite place, no harm intended; we'd like to know. Perhaps in a future edition we can share it with readers. This current selection has been based on our consistently good experiences . . . bad times happen to even well-managed establishments . . . that's what makes them human, and us forgiving. But continued offenses quickly eliminate them from our collection.

Even if cooking is not your "bag," I hope you will regard this book as a visit to an over 200-year-old city and its environs. San Diego is a paradox . . . very old and yet new. It is known as the "City in Motion." And, as if San Diego were all California in miniature scale, it has snow-capped mountains, arid lands, fertile valleys, moderate and extreme temperatures, grazing areas for fattening cattle and a seaport for fresh fish and shellfish. Restaurants run the gamut too, and those listed here are dedicated to satisfying every palate persuasion.

Some restaurants are known for their *Holiday* Magazine Awards, others for the best Margaritas in town or a salad fit for the gods, and many keep a steady clientele because of a particular ethnic cuisine. Whatever their charisma, it is anticipated that through this book you'll find it . . . in your kitchen or at one of these restaurants.

This recipe collection is an illustration of San Diego's

great restaurants and the art of its chefs. Although most of the recipes could hardly be called a cinch to prepare, neither are all of them complicated. The ordinary man or woman with a basic cooking know-how will be able to follow the instructions, which I have simplified as much as possible. Some recipes are easier than apple pie (which I don't consider particularly easy!) and may be turned out well by a novice. But bear in mind these are dining-out recipes, created to satisfy peoples' tastes when visiting restaurants. Remember, that's where you try to order what is not the weekly pattern of menus at home; so try these dishes as special ones for the family or on the occasion of your best-foot-forward company dinners. Don't be intimidated by lengthy recipes, for most of them are a matter of stages of preparation, with quick last minute procedures as restaurants must do.

Wherever possible I have lightened the load of what I considered unnecessary time and effort spent on ingredients or methods, and I hope the chefs will forgive me this transgression. Today's convenience foods are often used to speed up a prolonged recipe if they do not recognizably alter the flavors. If a recipe has required local ingredients, perhaps unavailable nationally, we have taken the liberty of substituting the next best thing. And we are confident that if you follow directions carefully, you will turn out a superb dish with a master's touch.

This book also proves that in 1972 many restaurants do serve quality, not pre-fab or instant dishes, and most small or grand restaurants are owner-operated . . . the better for them, and the better for us, the customers.

Dining out should be a happy experience. Culinary comparisons are what Bob and I like, don't you? The diversity you might expect in California's number two city ranges from kooky and do-it-yourself organic food restaurants to ceremonious, decorous dining rooms. So it is with the extraordinary recipes in this book, a little of everything, the sources varying from a unique drive-in to posh private clubs. Only the chef-size quantities of the recipes have been altered to suit domestic proportions.

To familiarize you with the vicinity of the restaurants there are full color photos of San Diego's best known areas, and there is a map to aid in pinpointing directions. Even San Diegans may find some eye-opening facts about their own community's products in the chapter on San Diego Cornucopia; and perhaps they'll be strangers no more to the very good vintners in San Diego County and nearby Baja California. These wineries boast a proud heritage as well as choice grapes.

And in case you have been wondering, the book earned it's name from a restaurant menu. As such it offers you the sybaritic experience of dining in many famous restaurants . . . at home. Our era is bursting with creativity, and for hobby-oriented people with more and more free time cooking is a new dimension. It's not unusual to blend ethnic cuisines or other food combinations any more, so although some recipes include suggested accompaniments, if you prefer a different go-with dish, forget the rules! Choose it freely, the Contents are assembled for you as a Bill of Fare.

June Crosby's
SAN DIEGO FARE

Super Antojitos

Most snacks are just a temporary stuffing for the tummy, but not super *antojitos*. In Tijuana the place for quick Mexican delicacies is Super Antojitos (snacks). There you can have a wide variety of foods, often adding up to a full meal.

There are two Super Antojitos in Tijuana, but I favor the one on Avenida Revolucion. It has character, you might say. It's a decided cut above the usual coffee shop U.S.A....floors are of pinkish brown marble tiles brought in from Tecali in the state of Puebla, wood on the interior is cut from the dark coco of Mexico's jungle, and the double front doors were hand-carved in Tijuana from single pieces of wood. The waitresses wear costumes from Southern Mexico, rarely seen up north, and the whole impression is of a place away south of the border. Early Aztec Indian mythology and religion have been introduced in the interior design. Stylized images of the Sun God, Tecatlipoca (Smoking Mirror), presumed responsible for ripening the harvest, are to be seen in many places. One is on the elaborate and very large menu. (If it were a little smaller, I might suggest menu snatching for the scene on the cover depicts the Aztecs and their pyramid city near the present Mexico City, with Tecatlipoca pointing a direction to the Indians.)

It's all very imaginative, and hard to believe that this inspiration sprung from a burning desire to taste familiar foods. Yet that's how it happened. When Señor Lecuga brought his family from the southern city of Villa Juarez, Mexico, they missed their native dishes so much that he finally decided to invest his entire savings and take the plunge in the restaurant business. That was ten years ago; now he has two flourishing restaurants and his family works to keep them that way.

10

It was a good move. This is one of the cleanest, shiniest stainless steel kitchens in Tijuana. The chefs prepare every bit of ground meat and sauce ingredients from the beginning, and Señor Lecuga believes this is one reason he has been successful. Another is people. Often people have an "I'm not sure what I want to eat, but I want something" feeling, and antojitos are the answer.

At this writing there are two Super A's, but in another year or so Señor Lecuga and his son, Caesar, plan to have a third restaurant down in Tecatlipoca's territory, in Mexico City. If so, I hope the Sun God showers them with as good a harvest as they have had in Tijuana's super snack restaurants.

Quesadillas are Mexican 'tween meal snacks, or in the smaller version, tasty appetizers. Basically they are turnovers made with unbaked corn tortillas, stuffed with varying goodies, then deep fried to a golden hue. Some rainy day try these super antojitos (snacks) from Super Antojitos restaurant.

QUESADILLAS
Corn Tortillas:
2 cups corn flour (masa harina*)
1/2 cup flour
1/2 tablespoon baking powder
1/4 teaspoon salt
1/2 to 1 cup milk

Mix dry ingredients together thoroughly; add one-half

---

*Masa (corn paste) harina (flour) is used in making tamales, tortillas, etc., as well as for thickening chiles, soups or gravies. It's origin is Mexican and it is available in supermarkets in all southwestern states. In other states it may be purchased in Spanish or Puerto Rican specialty stores. There is no suitable substitute for this food product. White cornmeal is made from fresh, green corn and masa is prepared from dry old white corn; the consistency between cornmeal and masa harina is also different.

13

cup milk, then continue to add milk until stiff but pliable dough is formed. Divide dough into 24 pieces for 4-inch quesadillas or 48 tiny amounts for appetizers. Tortilla making hint: slit side seams of a 1 gallon size plastic food storage bag; lay the opened bag on bread board. Place one piece of dough on inside half of bag; cover dough with outer half of bag and roll each tortilla with a rolling pin between the plastic surfaces to a round shape and paper thin thickness. When done, gently remove and set out on wax paper on kitchen counter.Cover with wax paper until ready to stuff and deep fry.

Stuffing:
*1 pound ground beef or 2 cups cooked, boned and
    chopped chicken, fish (tuna or shrimp)
    or leftover meat*
Salt to taste
1/2 onion, finely chopped and 1 clove garlic, minced
*1 can (4 ounces) diced green chiles or
    2/3 cup chili relish or salsa jalapeña*
2 cups diced (or grated) Monterey jack cheese
Oil for frying
Quacamole (optional), see Index
The above ingredients except oil and guacamole may be combined in whatever amounts you desire; these amounts are merely suggested as guides. (Other ingredients are used for stuffing in Mexico but are not so readily available in our U.S. markets, so they have not been recommended.) Place layered stuffing of about a tablespoon of meat with salt to taste, 1 teaspoon onion and garlic mixture, 1/2 teaspoon chiles and 1 teaspoon diced or grated cheese on one 4-inch tortilla. Fold over; pinch seal edges (use toothpicks for added security), return to counter and cover until all are in readiness to deep fry. In a large, deep heavy pot heat oil over medium high temperature to 400°. Deep fry a few quesadillas until golden, remove, drain on platter covered with paper towels. Keep hot in 200° oven until all are ready to serve. (The fillings keep hot for quite awhile.) Serve with guacamole, refried

beans, or a salad; or serve as small appetizers. Makes 24 four-inch snacks or 48 two-inch appetizers.

Note: These may also be pan-fried, but I think the results are better when deep fried as Super A's recommends. They may be prepared ahead of time and fried when ready to serve.

"LA PERLA"

What could be better than a seafood restaurant with a sea view? La Perla is up high and on the beach, and its guests can easily become dolphin-watchers. Dolphins are not like migrating whales that only perform seasonally for watchers along the San Diego coastline. Whether the dolphins passing La Perla are there because those waters provide the best playground within miles, or whether some unknown fish trainer has programmed them to glide past between 1:00 and 2:00 P.M., I don't know. But should you care to eat a delicious seafood (about any kind of ocean type) meal and catch the dolphin performance at the same time, head for the beach and La Perla for a late lunch.

This is the Tijuana you probably never knew existed. Known as the Playas (beaches) de Tijuana, it is about six miles southwest of the town, just off the Carretera (highway) *Canyon del Sol* (Canyon of the Sun) to Ensenada. It's a new section, mostly catering to a clean house and apartment residential area of Tijuanans. The new bull arena is there too, should you be interested in a corredá, but otherwise you won't see many shops since it's not a tourist mecca. The clean beaches spread out to eternity, and the clear smog-free air is for deep breathing. If you miss the dolphins, there are always San Diego's Coronado Island and Cabrillo Point landmarks to fix your eyes on.

But, of course, there is more. La Perla's reputation is substantially seafood, especially seafood cocktails, lobster thermidor and clam chowder. You'll also find

15

unusual ocean fresh fish there, up from San Felipe and the Gulf of Baja California, such specialties as octopus, totuava and caguama (sea turtle). They also have a good selection of charcoal-broiled meats if you prefer.

La Perla is a mere five years old, and is a family operated restaurant run by Señor José Oceguera, his wife and four children. It is extremely popular as a seasonal gathering place for aficionados after the corredás, and there the brave bulls and toreadors are rehashed conversationally. The restaurant is quiet, relaxed and informal, a good retreat from whatever. The ocean makes it easy to become a window viewer, and the peace of being away from the city pace is like a brief vacation.

Clam chowder is delicious, whether Manhattan or New England in style, but in California it may take a connoisseur to distinguish our Western clams from their popular eastern counterparts. La Perla's Clam Chowder is every bit as good as the New York City version, and the clams are strictly Pacific...they never even knew there was another ocean!

CLAM CHOWDER

24 scrubbed clams or 1 can (8 ounces) minced sea clams
Water
2 tablespoons oil
1 1/2 medium onions, finely chopped
1 can (15 ounces) tomato sauce
1 can (12 ounces) clam juice
1 cup finely chopped celery
1 bay leaf
1 tablespoon A-1 sauce
Salt and pepper to taste
2 medium boiling potatoes, peeled and diced

Place clams with just enough water to cover in a deep heavy soup pot. Steam covered over medium-high heat until all clams open. Remove clams; strain juice through wet cheesecloth and reserve. Slit stomachs, discard con-

16

tents and rinse clams; chop them into small pieces and reserve. If canned clams are used, strain juice and reserve it to add to water or chicken broth later; reserve clams separately. Over medium heat in same soup pot heat oil and sauté onions until limp. Stir in tomato sauce and both canned and reserved clam juice. (If canned clams were used add water or chicken broth to make 3 cups liquid). Add celery, carrots and bay leaf. Simmer covered over low heat for one and one-half hours. Add A-1 sauce and check for additional seasoning. Add potatoes and simmer uncovered until potatoes are tender (about one-half hour). Add steamed clams; simmer 4 minutes more. Serve piping hot in soup bowls with a variety of crackers. Makes about 8 cups soup or 4 to 6 bowls.

Note: Oyster soup can be prepared by using this same method, substituting 24 oysters for the clams.

Del Mar
Thoroughbred Club

I guess you could call San Diego the relaxed county. The resorts, sports, spas and the tourist business are on a large scale, and casual; the prevailing attitude and climate are more expansive. For this reason Del Mar Turf Club has often been called the Saratoga of the West. In no way does that imply that it looks like the eastern track; it's purely that the surrounding influence makes it a place to see old friends in a sort of country fair atmosphere.

Most Del Mar race-goers have known the track for several years, perhaps not all as long as I (because of married life and kinship) but we have, many of us, watched the "little foal" develop through awkward periods and several immature stages to a horsey and dignified coming-of-age. It took perhaps ten years to get Del Mar out of the podunk class, but there were a lot of helping hands. Bing and his friends Pat O'Brien, Bill Quigley, brother Everett Crosby, and Oliver Hardy together lured the right horses, purses and glamor of celebrities to sparkle on the mile track and in the mission-style clubhouse. And from 1938 on Bing sang a newly recorded song written especially for Del Mar (title coined by Mrs. Herb Polesie, music by James V. Monaco, and collaborating on lyrics, Johnny Burke): "Where the Turf Meets the Surf" is still the friendly opener and closer to every racing day, and with Bing's happy-go-lucky voice you can't go away mad even if you're a loser. It also helps to know that Monaco and Burke collaborated on "Pennies from Heaven!"

There were other factors. Photo-Chart was first used at Del Mar and ever since it has determined with unquestionable accuracy each horse crossing the finish line. The Del Mar Futurity and later the Del Mar Debutante brought attention to two-year-olds in the horse circuit. The off-season Del Mar Yearling Sales made it one of the three leading yearling sales markets in the United States. Through all this development, it underwent several management altercations and changes, and then the war blackout and with it a military installation. Recently Del Mar had a new lease renewal and the new board of directors are all horse owners, except for one attorney. With every step it is going forward.

Del Mar has retained all the good and made it better. There have been extensive improvements made to the infield, including elaborate landscaping with several graceful palm trees. But basically Del Mar is a pretty setting, with its Spanish colonial buildings and the clubhouse similar to the Iturbide Palace in Mexico City. Delightful sea breezes still continue to surprise visiting turfers with the need for a wrap by the last race. And it is one of the friendliest places in the country to enjoy the sport of kings. In thirty plus years the food and the service at the Turf Club have paralleled the prevailing track conditions...clear and fast and the food has been about perfect. (Indeed in all this time they've only had about one-half dozen "off" days of racing.) The new regime promises a new leaf in Del Mar's pages, but what's good

18

will remain. There will still be the popular Mexican plate and the glorious Fresh Fruit Salad for luncheons, and the Saturday night dinners will continue; but this season you'll be talking of the new chef and his distinctive menu along with recounting your Daily Double and Exacta winners.

You may have to fight your way in to win a table and a chance at the Daily Double, but with delicious foods to savor, and pleasant weather, and friendly folk, Del Mar is a good place to count ten. It's different from other (city) tracks, it's in that *relaxed county* of San Diego.

For a cool, refreshing yet zesty mid day meal, Gazpacho is the answer. A cup of Gazpacho overflows with vitamins, as a quick glance at the list of ingredients will tell you. Better still, Executive Chef Marcel Kernane's recipe is so good you'll delight in directing this chunky but liquid "salad" towards your tummy.

GAZPACHO VALENCIENNE
1 cucumber, peeled, seeded and diced
3/4 medium onion, diced
2 medium tomatoes, peeled, seeded and diced
1 stalk celery, diced
1 to 2 cloves garlic, minced or crushed, to taste
2 sweet green peppers, seeded and diced
3 tablespoons parsley, finely chopped
1 teaspoon fresh basil, finely chopped,
    or 1/2 teaspoon dried basil
2 teaspoons finely chopped, fresh oregano,
    or 1 teaspoon dried oregano
1/3 cup olive oil
3 cups tomato juice
1 teaspoon Worcestershire sauce
1 tablespoon soy sauce
Dash of Tabasco, or to taste
1 1/2 tablespoons salt, to taste
1 teaspoon white pepper
1/2 cup or more garlic-flavored bread croutons, optional

SALADS

Prepare all vegetables. Combine in large bowl with remaining ingredients, except croutons. Blend with wire whisk until mixed. Refrigerate 4 hours or more until well chilled; serve in chilled crystal cups if available. Garnish with croutons if desired. Makes 8 cups or 4-6 servings, depending on size of soup bowls or cups; this soup is often served in large bowls since it is a meal by itself.

Caesar's

Tijuana

Caesar's is one of Tijuana's oldest and best-known restaurants, still serving a salad that was originated there in 1927 by Alex and Caesar Cardini. Alex, a former Italian pilot in World War I, created his "Aviator's Salad" dedicating it to his good friends at Rockwell Field, North Island, San Diego. In forty-five years the salad has made history as Caesar's Salad; but Tijuana is where it happened ... no matter what anybody says!

It was back in 1927, when Tijuana was in its heyday. Then it was the popular escape for Californians dodging prohibition in the States. Tijuana offered action, bargains and good food at Paul and Alex's place. Old-timers will tell you it was so good the restaurant drew Admirals, Generals, movie stars from Hollywood, and other prominent social figures including the then Governor Abelardo Rodriguez of Baja California, who later became President of Mexico. They all spread the word, and returned as often as possible.

The partners, Paul Maggiora and Alex Cardini, eventually parted company, and Alex joined up with his brother Caesar. Finally with the increasing popularity of the Alex-Caesar Cardini Salad, the word people seemed to remember was Caesar, so the restaurant and salad became known as Caesar's.

To this day Alex is such a firm believer in his salad invention that he has a standing offer open to anyone

20

who can substantiate any contrary proof to the origin of the recipe. (He's not fretting over it either!) He backs up his claim with a wager of $1,000 to $1,000. Are there any takers?

Caesar's restaurant is in the Jai Lai area, which is convenient if you're on foot, but not in your huraches, please. After all, you're there to see and taste a replica of the real thing, so dress like a devoted gourmet who knows a bit of the history of the original Aviator's Salad. Remember how ceremoniously some northern restaurants prepare this specialty when they make their version? Well doesn't the real Caesar's deserve the same respect? Right Alex?

THE ORIGINAL ALEX-CAESAR CARDINI ROMAINE SALAD

1 cup French bread croutons
1/3 cup olive oil
2 cloves garlic
1 to 2 teaspoons anchovy paste
1 bunch romaine, inside leaves
Salt and pepper to taste
1/4 cup freshly grated Parmesan cheese
1 (1 minute) coddled or soft cooked egg
Juice of 1 lemon
1 teaspoon Worcestershire sauce

Crisp croutons in a skillet containing 2 tablespoons olive oil flavored with a split clove of garlic; stir in anchovy paste. Rub wooden bowl with second split clove of garlic. Place rinsed romaine, dried, cut into bite-sized pieces and chilled, in bowl. Sprinkle with salt and pepper. Sprinkle with remaining oil and grated cheese. Add croutons. Break egg directly over greens; or into small bowl, beating a few seconds gently with a fork then pouring over greens. Sprinkle Worcestershire and lemon juice over greens. Toss thoroughly but lightly so as not to bruise. Greens should be well-coated, but no excess liquid should remain in bowl. Makes 4 servings.

23

Tijuana

Tijuana is the point of origin for two very popular dishes...one, the Caesar Salad, the other, Carne Asada al Carbon. Carne Asada is the tasty filet steak that is marinated, then charcoal-broiled or sautéed to doneness and served with Salsa Fresca (fresh tomato sauce) and whatever else pleases the chef. Carne Asada is a Victors restaurant "first," and needless to say, you'll find it most properly done at Victors on Boulevard Aqua Caliente. There have been several newspaper and magazine articles written about this specialty and Victor Rubio, the owner, has even given some thought to writing a book on the subject of the many ways of preparing carne asada. Almost every restaurant in Tijuana prepares some version and many San Diego restaurants have also adopted variations of this recipe. However, don't hold your breath for the book, for Victor has other interests.

Today it's hard to imagine Victor M. Rubio as a bus boy and odd jobber, but that's the way he started some seventeen years ago. Then he had the foresight to see the need for an unusual restaurant offering a limited but desirable menu of Mexican dishes accompanied by some American standards, and that's what led to the construction of the sombrero on Boulevard Aqua Caliente. This large Mexican hat is the architecture of Victors restaurant, and inside is his Carne Asada Room. This was his testing ground, where through trial and error he succeeded in learning the restaurant business.

There is also a very different downtown Victors. It's a cafeteria and caters to rapid self-service; whereas Victors Sombrero is small and intimate, with only about ten tables and quiet, attentive service. Quite a contrast.

Whether dining as a couple or in a group, you will be fascinated watching the preparation of their romaine salad. This delicious companion piece to the carne asada is mixed at each table. Salads are not presented to guests as pre-assembled piles of leaves tossed onto plates in the kitchen. At Victors, food and service go together.

In fact, Victor Rubio learned so much through his early restaurant years that he even became a stock broker on the side, advising on Mexican securities and investments. And he should know about investments, for he's not a single goal type man; in each enterprise he improves the status quo with a different idea. Maybe before too many people forget the source of his carne asada recipe, it should be named Victors Steak and join with the fame of Caesar Salad.

All salads don't have to snap at you to be good...this one doesn't, it's delicate, and it is definitely good. It is close to being a Caesar salad, but only because it has almost the same ingredients. This will please you with it's subtlety; on other occasions you may prefer the assertiveness of it's familiar amigo, "The Caesar."

ROMAINE SALAD

1 clove garlic, peeled and sliced
1/2 cup olive oil
2 heads romaine
Salt
1/4 teaspoon freshly grated black pepper
1/2 teaspoon Worcestershire sauce
1 teaspoon A-1 steak sauce
3 drops Tabasco sauce
2 eggs, slightly beaten
1 teaspoon mayonnaise
Juice of 1/2 lemon
1/2 cup grated Queso Cotja* or Parmesan cheese

Begin by putting garlic in olive oil overnight or 8-12 hours ahead of use. Break romaine leaves into about 2-inch pieces and rinse in cold water. Dry on paper toweling and roll to crisp it in refrigerator. At salad preparation time, remember the secret of it is the continued mixing

25

of ingredients as they are added. First sprinkle a dash of salt over leaves in a large salad mixing bowl. Repeat process with pepper and sauces. Pour garlic oil (discard garlic slices) over salad greens. To slightly beaten eggs add mayonnaise. Pour egg mixture over greens. Squeeze lemon, strain and pour juice over salad. Finally sprinkle grated cheese over and toss through thoroughly. Serve at once. Makes 4 ample servings.

Note: The recipe may be prepared by combining the ingredients for the salad dressing in a small bowl or jar and beating with a fork to mix. Later you may toss through salad as recommended above; but if so, sprinkle cheese through greens after dressing has been poured over it.

*Queso Cotja is a medium strong hard Mexican cheese. In strength and taste it falls somewhere between Romano and Parmesan.

Cheese and garlic and sour dough bread are excellent companions. Try this recipe from Victors in Tijuana with their Romaine Salad.

GARLIC BREAD
1 clove garlic, peeled and sliced
2 tablespoons corn oil
2 tablespoons butter
1 small French or sour dough loaf bread
2 tablespoons Parmesan cheese
Paprika

Prepare garlic in oil and leave overnight or 8-12 hours ahead of use. Preheat oven to 350°. Melt butter over very low heat; add to oil. Discard garlic slices. Spread mixture on thick slices of bread. Sprinkle slices with cheese, then sprinkle with paprika. Bake about 3 minutes only on a cookie sheet. Serve hot wrapped in a linen napkin. Makes 6 or more servings.

These egg noodles are given a very special treatment. After cooking they are tossed with dairy products three times . . . hence the Italian name, noodles in triple-buttered style! Delicious.

FETTUCCINE AL TRIPLICE BURRO (BOCACCIO'S)
1 package (10 ounces) fettuccine
4 to 6 quarts boiling water
1 tablespoon salt
1/4 pound butter
2 tablespoons water
2 tablespoons milk
1/2 cup grated Parmesan cheese

Drop fettuccine noodles into rapidly boiling salted water. Cook to al dente (chewy) stage, about 8 minutes; 10 minutes if softer noodles are preferred. Strain noodles in colander. In noodle pot melt butter over low heat and let it bubble up, but not brown. Pour noodles back into pot and over medium heat mix well with butter. Stir with 2 forks; let bubble up; add water. Stir and let bubble up again; add milk. Toss with cheese. Pour noodles into heated bowl and serve. More Parmesan cheese may be passed with fettuccine. Makes 4 ample servings.

TORTILLA FLATS

Nuzzled deep in the minds of John Steinbeck fans is the little Mexican community he created for his novel *Tortilla Flat*. It was dismal and grimy; you almost wanted to brush off the 'dobe dust while thumbing the pages. Steinbeck always showed us the seamy side of life and made it real for the reader.

Tortilla Flats in San Diego is real all right. The architect and owner created a remarkable duplication booktown, but without the desparate depression and the smell of dirt. Theirs is a humble village of brick streets and adobe casas nestling under clear blue San Diego skies. What seems altogether incredible is that Tortilla

27

Flats is smack in the middle of Mission Valley. Many of you may have passed it at some time or another without even knowing this other world existed so close at hand. Tortilla Flats restaurant brings out all the color in Steinbeck's novel. Set as it is, among the trees and with buildings planned as if on a village street, Tortilla Flats has been arranged to offer diners variety in seating location. On good warm days there's nothing better than the terrace room, but the patio is a perfect spot too. When it's cool, step inside the adobe house or the hacienda and enjoy the colorful Mexican decor.

You'll find the waiters and waitresses are young and pleasant, and their "buenos días" sounds sincere. And why not? Undoubtedly they can express themselves without rancor in this pristine Tortilla Flats. Besides, they look flamboyant and happy in their traditional Mexican costumes. It's easy to become entranced in this complete atmosphere. It makes you feel as if you have taken a quick trip to a Disney-type setting, and yet all the while you are almost in the center of San Diego . . . and befitting the name Tortilla Flats, the restaurant is situated on one of the flattest spots in town.

Naturally you would expect to find Mexican food, and so it is, authentic and delicious, and served with wines or beer to chase some of the *caliente* (hot) foods down. But Mexican menus are not just hot chiles, there are also many bland dishes that are good to savor.

So let the seamy side rest in Steinbeck's Monterey Flat and enjoy the smooth restaurant operation that recalls the good, not the bad. Come away with me to this place that I know. It has character and reminds me an awful lot of the book John Steinbeck wrote.

Chiles Rellenos (pronounced chee-lehs rreh-yeh-nohs) or stuffed peppers are one of the best known dishes served by Mexican restaurants in America. They are usually stuffed with cheese and often have the full name of Chiles Rellenos con Queso. Tortilla Flats makes them the best I know.

CHILES RELLENOS

*1 can (7 ounces) peeled California green chiles or
6 to 8 fresh California or Pablano green chiles,
peeled
1/2 pound Monterey jack cheese
About 1/2 cup flour
Salad oil for frying
3 eggs
1 tablespoon water
3 tablespoons flour
1/4 teaspoon salt*

If chiles are not canned and peeled prepare by holding a chili pepper over a flame to broil it, or by placing it on a surface of medium hot electric range unit until it has become spotted from the heat. Remove and wrap in a towel or heavy paper bag to let steam for 15 minutes, then peel skin, slit chiles lengthwise, remove core and seeds. Cut cheese into about 1/2-inch-wide and 1/2-inch-thick sizes, with length about 1 inch shorter than the chiles themselves. Stuff each chili with a slice of cheese. To hold chili together you may need toothpicks. Roll chiles in flour. Heat about 1 to 1 1/2 inches of oil in large frying pan over medium heat. Separate eggs; beat whites until soft peaks are formed. Beat yolks with water; add flour and salt. Beat to mix thoroughly; fold whites into yolks. Dip stuffed chiles into fluffy batter, hold by stem end and drop in oil or with the aid of a spoon place each on saucer and slide into hot oil. Do not crowd chiles in pan. Baste with hot oil; gently turn using a spatula and fork. Fry only until golden, about 3 or 4 minutes on each side. Drain on paper towels. Makes 4 to 6 servings (approximately 8 stuffed Chiles.)

CASA DE PICO

There's something new in Old Town. It's a kind of "farmer's market," designed in a Mexican plaza setting, filled with international shops and an indoor-outdoor restaurant, the Casa de Pico...a fine new Mexican cuisine dining room.

The Spanish Colonial architecture of long ago has been restored, with generous areas devoted to space, today's precious commodity. The plaza or inner courtyard is a pleasure to stroll around, and while there, you feel as if time were of no importance. It's too clean, too fresh, to be a movie set, yet you feel it could be, because of its perfect layout. The tiled shop walkways, the courtyard blooming with flowers, some growing, others vying for attention in their oversized, vivid colors of paper Mexican art. And a gazebo-bandstand *a centro* with dancing space for special celebrations. There's even a flower market with colorful canvas sky draperies where you feel you must be on foreign soil as you barter over flowers or plants. The Bazaar del Mundo, as this whole new and interesting place is called, is the historical present, the Epitomy of early California.

Actually the Casa de Pico restaurant is located right where General Pío Pico, who was California's civil governor during the Mexican era, built his hacienda. I think he'd be pleased.

The restaurant is architecturally restored to the colonial look and it features hand-painted designs on the walls and ceilings. On balmy days the courtyard is festive and beautiful; definitely the place to eat and see and take a hiatus. The menu consists of classic Mexican dishes with a select assortment of American entrées, and there's a choice of domestic or Mexican beer and wine.

Before or after dining it's fun to wander around in this modern version of famous market places and bazaars of Spain and Mexico. It's dangerous too; there's so much to be attracted to. The Design Center popping with home items from furniture to crystal; The Gallery with (what else?) art of all sorts; The Candle Shop with fascinating forms of flares for favored friends; Paja, the place to find straws of all descriptions; Antelline's Fruit Bazaar for dried fruits, preserves and confections; Libros, one shop that carries an international collection of books; The Gifted Hand for fine Polish folk art; Artes de Mexico for arts and crafts from far below the border; Gusterman Silversmiths for hand-wrought jewelry to think about; the Flower Market a blooming pleasure, Marimekko with all manner of things from Finland; Whirling Logs housing American Indian arts and crafts; Lindas Ropas with clothes and accessories that are just a bit different; the Farmer's Market itself with fresh produce, delicatessen and international foods; plus Geppetto's for the kiddies toys and clothes, and La Panderia for food delicacies, such as Mexican breads, pastries, coffee and hot chocolate, to snack on or to take home. That's what's new and old in Old Town. It's to be seen and enjoyed and it's waiting for you.

If you like scrambled eggs with anything, you'll like Huevos Revueltos at Casa de Pico. It is a dish of eggs and a bit of this and that. The this and that add just the flavors you will like to spruce up plain scrambled eggs. Try them for an easy lunch or brunch.

HUEVOS REVUELTOS
1 tablespoon each butter and oil
1/2 cup finely chopped onion
1 clove garlic, crushed (optional)
1 medium tomato, peeled, deseeded and chopped
2 tablespoons (canned) diced green chiles
1 tablespoon finely chopped parsley
6 eggs
1 tablespoon cream
1/2 teaspoon salt

In a skillet over medium heat melt butter and oil. Add

onion and garlic; cook until limp. Add tomato; cook until most of liquid has evaporated. Add chiles and parsley. Beat eggs with cream and salt and turn into skillet. Scramble, mixing ingredients well, to desired doneness. Serve immediately with refried beans, hot sour dough rolls or toasted tortillas. Makes 4 ample servings.

If you yearn to get away from it all, don't worry about seasons, directions or what to wear . . . The Mad Greek brings you a complete change of scene without leaving the country. For a moment you'll say, "This man Jean Claude Marengo is utterly mad!" as you step inside his taverna. You can't imagine the varied, unusual and beautiful Balkan 'trappings' he has so artfully put to use in decorating his restaurant, and words do seem empty describers.

Yet, here goes. Picture ceilings festooned with subtle lighting from brass lanterns, and walls (would you believe?) literally wrapped in soft fur skins, and corners everywhere filled with tambourines and bouzoukias, or gorgeous copper pieces. It's a mêlée, but moods matter. Somehow you just know you have floated across the Mediterranean, disembarked on one of those stark, white islands, and sought out a narrow, stoney street, which led you to this warm and festive cafe.

It's not so, but it is convincing. There is music too, ebbing from somewhere, and occasionally the *Theme From Zorba the Greek* adds to the credibility. Waiters and barmaids are costumed in authentic Greek folk garments, much too fine to wear hustling in and out of the kitchen. With so much to see, you can never be bored with the astonishing surroundings, but Marengo offers more . . . Greek floor shows. Each performance electrifies the place with intense strumming of bouzoukias, singing of Greek songs, and gyrations of an agile belly dancer, whose vitality seems endless.

As you might expect, the food is 90% Greek; but, if you are unfamiliar with this cuisine and skeptical too, you'll find security (oddly enough) in The Mad Greek Special! It's an exquisite filet mignon with potatoes smothered in white sauce. Otherwise this is the occasion for sampling "different" Greek taste sensations, with flavors such as mint, oregano and lemon in exotic combinations. Moussaka is another almost national dish and always my choice for an entrée. Since Greece is so very far away, Marengo's restaurant lets me savor this dish in realistic surroundings, while still only a stone's throw from home.

Moussaka (pronounced moo-sa-ka') is a strange name, but the ingredients are not. It is composed of layers of eggplant, meat, cheese and Béchamel Sauce baked in casserole. If you don't take to eggplant, I doubt you'd detect it's presence, for there are many seasonings and textures to distract. So, some wild moment cook up The Mad Greek's Moussaka and see for yourself.

MOUSSAKA
1 medium eggplant
Water & 2 tablespoons salt
Flour
1/2 cup each, oil & butter
2 onions, chopped
1 pound ground beef
1/3 cup pine nuts, optional
1/8 teaspoon ground oregano
1/8 teaspoon ground cinnamon
Pinch of ground cloves
Pinch of ground allspice
Seasoning salt & pepper, to taste
1/4 cup chopped fresh parsley
1 cup Mavrodaphne (Greek wine) or other sweet red wine
1 1/4 cups freshly grated Kefaloteri (Greek cheese) or
*   Romano or Parmesan*

2 *large tomatoes, peeled and sliced*
4 *to* 6 *large fresh mushrooms, sliced*
6 *strips bacon, fried and crumbled*
About 3 1/2 cups Béchamel Sauce, see Index

Peel eggplant; slice in 1/2-inch rounds. Cover with water and salt in bowl; let stand 15 minutes. Drain; rinse under cold water, pat dry with paper toweling. Dredge with flour. Sauté over medium heat in large skillet with 3 tablespoons each of oil and butter. Remove slices to platter. In same skillet, sauté onions until limp. Add meat; stir and cook 5 minutes. Add pine nuts, sprinkle in seasonings and parsley; add wine and stir. Simmer uncovered over low heat until liquid is absorbed. In small skillet heat remaining oil and butter; sauté mushrooms until golden. Set aside. Prepare Béchamel Sauce; cool slightly. Grease bottom and sides of 9 x 13-inch baking dish. Place in it a layer of eggplant, spread with meat mixture, sprinkle with 1 cup cheese, add tomatoes in a layer, then mushrooms. Pour Béchamel Sauce over all. Sprinkle with remaining cheese and bacon. Bake about 45 minutes in preheated 375° oven. To serve, cut in squares. Makes 4 to 6 ample servings.

Note: This dish improves on standing overnight. It is excellent for planning ahead dinners. Cover with foil and reheat in 300° oven. Remove foil after 30 minutes, bake 5 to 10 minutes without a cover. Serve hot or lukewarm.

Anthony's Fish Grottos

Like Topsy, Anthony's Fish Grottos "just grew." I'm sure in 1946, right after the war, Mrs. Catherine Ghio never dreamed her tiny fish cafe on the San Diego Embarcadero would one day become three fine restaurants. Yet today there's a brand new one at the Wharf and two more, scattered throughout the county, at La Jolla and La Mesa, and primarily because of the excellent food Mrs. Ghio originally served. Her recipes still are menu specialties that customers return again and again to relish. Her family is another reason for Anthony's success. Mrs. Ghio's sons Anthony and Todd and son-in-law Roy Weber started as mother's helpers and eventually became a team of competent management. They work together for the three restaurants in their various capacities, be they accounting and purchasing, management, or developing new recipes and supervising the kitchens. It's a family affair.

The name Fish Grottos also "just grew," probably as a result of the architecturally designed cave-like entrance to the La Jolla restaurant. Once inside Anthony's Fish Grotto in La Jolla, it's like sitting in a tree-top with a bird's eye view of the Pacific. And in La Mesa a completely different atmosphere is created, for Anthony's is on the fringes of a tranquil lake surrounded by towering eucalyptus trees. The third and newest location is almost back where it all started...on the wharf. This building is simple and functional in design, and it blends so well with the Wharf that one feels it has been there all along. The dining room interior is done in rough wood paneling and leather, with some details reminiscent of old sailing ships. Since the restaurant does extend out over the Bay waters, it doesn't take much imagination to feel you've embarked for somewhere. On another side of the building is a glassed-in outdoor terrace for standing or sitting while enjoying the convenience of the Oyster Bar and harbor view.

All three restaurants offer casual comfort, the same dependable menu, good service and quality. Particular attention has been given to planning menus and original recipes that will suit the customers' tastes and diets (they use over 50% polyunsaturated oils in food preparation). Anthony's even considers the customers' purses, and offers a fine menu at moderate prices. In San Diego County, fish and Anthony's are synonymous!

Needless to say, Mrs. Catherine Ghio's recipes are always popular, but it's her son Todd who deserves credit for the easy and excellent recipe for Prawns International (large shrimp may be used equally well). I serve it family-style from a big casserole with everyone helping himself, and I have plenty of napkins available. It has now become one of my husband's favorite seafood dishes; but I can never decide which he enjoys most, dunking the shrimp or the French bread in the superb garlic-flavored sauce, or the sauce itself?

PRAWNS INTERNATIONAL
About 10 prawns or 16 large shrimp
1/3 cup butter
2/3 cup olive oil
6 large garlic cloves, crushed
2 teaspoons chopped cilantro, optional*
2 tablespoons dry sherry wine
2 teaspoons salt
1 teaspoon monosodium glutamate or Accent

Prepare prawns or shrimp: rinse, slit down back with sharp knife, cut through shells and devein. Slice almost through meat to flatten shrimp, do not remove shells or feet (when cooked, the feet are chewy tidbits). Cover bottom of skillet about 1/4-inch deep with butter and olive oil. Place pan on range over medium heat. Add garlic, stir and cook lightly. Add prawns spread apart, meat side down, tails up. Cook over high heat (about 400° on an electric skillet) 5 minutes for shrimp, about 7 minutes for prawns. Stir and turn occasionally. Add cilantro, sherry, salt and monosodium glutamate to skillet; stir and mix around. Simmer a minute then pour entire mixture with prawns into a heated casserole (to serve family-style), or in individual dishes if you prefer. Shells are easily removed, and finger-eating is permissable. Heated, unbuttered French bread has never had a more delicious flavor than when it is dunked into the super-sauce of this dish. If you serve it with a tossed green salad and Italian dressing, you have a complete and unforgettable meal. Makes 3 to 4 servings.

*Cilantro, also known as coriander is a Mexican or Chinese type of parsley. Some people find it too pungent and prefer the American double-curled variety.

Boom Trenchard's FLARE PATH

The food is great, but perhaps more importantly, you'll leave "Boom's" satisfied that the visit had been a total experience. There's nothing comparable to it. This restaurant is an ingeniously designed aerospace museum, a memorabilia of great monetary and historical significance, built on land at old Lindbergh Field terminal, and occupying an excellent viewing position for arriving and departing airplanes . . . especially those sparrow-sized models that park nearby.

"Boom" Trenchard, for whom the restaurant was named, was not only the "father of the R.A.F.," but the "architect and patron saint of modern airpower." He was a physical and moral giant among men, endowed with vision and decision. Next to Churchill, England owes him the most for its survival. First Viscount Hugh Montague Trenchard, GCB, OM, GCVO, DSO, "Boom" to the men who followed and respected him (although he was never called that to his face), will live forever in the hearts of airmen throughout the world.

Okay, the history lesson is over. But, one more thing, if the young generation mentions the Sopwith "Camel" at "Boom's," remember you are talking about F-1's, otherwise known as the backbone of the R.A.F. fighter squadrons of World War I . . . not a pop musical group.

For this is "Aeroplane Town." Ever since the first glider was successfully flown by John Montgomery in 1883 and Charles Lindberg's "Spirit of St. Louis" was built and first flown here, "flying machines" have lined up for approaches to flare paths, just as jets line up for approaches now. The old and the new Lindbergh Field are centered in downtown San Diego and have brought to it the sight, sound and excitement of aviation. Now this unique six-level restaurant, poised on the edge of Runway 2-7, keeps that excitement aglow with its storehouse

SEAFOOD

of artifacts representing aviation from 1912 to 1945, and the role San Diego played in it.

Boom Trenchard's Flare Path Restaurant is only to be believed on sight. Fly in, walk or drive; or if you have your own plane, park at the old Lindbergh terminal side, but do spend some time. What grandiose dimensions it has, all the way from the underground replica of an English World War II bomb shelter (which they've turned into a fun-filled banquet room) up to the top level, called the Lone Eagle Lounge, which honors Charles A. Lindberg and offers a fantastic view of the new airport, the Harbor and the Navy carrier fleet anchorage!

Tour "Boom's," sit there and watch air traffic over cocktails, or simply take pleasure in the food. I think you'll come away saying Boom Trenchard's Flare Path was more than you expected.

For variety the chef changes the type of curry from lobster one day to shrimp the next, or crab, or lamb, or chicken, or mixed seafood. They're all fine unless you personally tune out on certain foods. My favorite is the combination Seafood Curry. With this dish comes rice pilaf, "Six-Boy" Condiments, and a delectable pineapple fritter. Never can figure out which part of Boom's curry dinner I like the best!

MIXED SEAFOOD CURRY

1/4 cup butter
1/4 cup chopped onion
1/4 cup chopped tart apple
1/4 cup chopped celery
2 1/2 tablespoons flour
1/2 to 2 teaspoons curry powder, to taste
1 1/2 cups chicken broth or bouillon
1/2 cup cream
1/2 teaspoon grated lemon peel
Dash of Tabasco sauce, optional
1/2 teaspoon ground ginger, optional

38

2 *tablespoons chutney, optional*
1 *teaspoon sherry wine, optional*
2 *cups peeled, deveined, cooked shrimp*
1 *cup cooked, diced lobster meat*
1 *cup steam cooked scallops*

Melt butter in a large skillet over medium heat; sauté onion, apple, and celery until limp. Stir flour and curry powder into skillet mixture. While constantly stirring, add broth slowly, then cream and lemon peel. Simmer until thoroughly blended and thickened, (about five minutes) over very low heat. If you wish a smooth sauce, strain it; if not, leave as is. If you wish to liven the sauce, add the optional ingredients. Pour the sauce over cooked seafood. Return to the stove, reheat over low heat, stirring slowly until seafood is piping hot. To serve, spoon curry sauce and seafood over a bed of hot rice. Offer condiments of currants, coconut, chutney, almonds (cashews or peanuts, if preferred), finely chopped green onions or scallions, and candied ginger. If you like, serve a pineapple fritter with this dinner; it makes a fresh yet delicate accent. Makes 4 servings.

Brigantine

When three young men put their heads together, they're bound to come up with some fresh ideas on "the establishment restaurant" theme. Naturally Mike and Lance Morton and Alan Crawford made their quota of beginner's mistakes, especially since their only claim to being restaurateurs was ownership of land; but, as if to compensate for their inexperience, just three years ago Lady Luck smiled on these bold self-starters in her own way.

The Brigantine's location, partly Point Loma and partly Shelter Island, has proved convenient; and its proximity to the yacht basin lent itself readily to a nautical

41

name hastily selected from a dictionary. Fortunately the trio hired key people to help them get off the ground, including a whizz of a bartender to create all types of refreshing "grog." They had the good sense to trim their sails on the menu with a limited galley selection of well-prepared fresh seafood and fine steaks at reasonable prices . . . plus notable house wines by the litre and foreign and domestic wines by the bottle. The Brig also boasts young efficient and friendly personnel.

With all of these positive signals flashing from 2912 Shelter Island Drive you might ask, "How come I haven't seen this restaurant before?" And rightly so . . . for how many restaurants are off the street, behind a liquor store and above a first floor storeroom? Before you go forming opinions, take a turn on this two-masted, square-rigged ship. Climb the darkish stairway to the cozy, nautical atmosphere of the "upper deck" where you'll find booths for intimate dining, or tables if you prefer. It's small and snug and filled with folks who have become habitúes after one visit. What brings them back? That's hard to pinpoint. Is it the home-made clam chowder and yummy hot French bread, the convivial ambience, or something else, such as undaunted youth being successful?

Cioppino is California's most famous contribution to the world's great seafood recipes. As the story goes, the origin was the invention of a fisherman who brought in his day's catch and made from it this delectable stew. There are as many versions of it as for bouillabaisse or gumbo. However, the Brig's Cioppino is one you'll want to earmark for frequent future use.

CIOPPINO

Fish Fumet:
1 pound fish (rock cod fish, preferably, or white fish), cut into pieces
1/2 pound fish heads and bones
1 quart water

1 1/2 tablespoons salt
1 1/2 teaspoons Accent (monosodium glutamate)
Greens from 1 celery top

Put all ingredients in large pot. Simmer covered for 1/2 hour. (Unlike meat or chicken stock, fish stock takes a very short time to cook). Strain and set aside. Makes about one quart stock.

Sauce:

1 1/4 medium-sized onions, chopped
1 stalk celery, chopped
4 cloves garlic, crushed or minced
2 tablespoons fresh snipped parsley or 1 1/2 teaspoons
    dry parsley flakes
1/2 cup olive oil
3 1/2 tablespoons red wine vinegar
3/4 cup burgundy wine
1 1/4 teaspoons allspice
1 tablespoon salt
1 pint (2 cups) water

Sauté vegetables in oil until limp. Add remaining ingredients and one quart fish fumet; simmer 1 1/2 hours, until thickened.

Seafood:

1 pound fresh or frozen raw shrimp, peeled and deveined
3/4 pound (12 ounces) fresh or frozen scallops
12 raw clams, scrubbed
1 pound King or Dungeness crab legs, cracked
1 pound boned white fish (bass, halibut or cod), cut in
    chunks
6 lemon wedges

Divide seafood equally into 6 individual ovenproof casseroles (with covers). Or place seafood on bottom of one large deep casserole or baked bean pot, if individual containers are unavailable. Fill ovenproof pots to brim with prepared Sauce. Add more water, if needed. Cover and bake in preheated 450° oven for 20 to 30 minutes. Serve with bowls for discarding bones and shells. In addition to your preference in paper or linen napkins for this by hand, soup spoon and seafood fork dish, it is nice to offer Wash 'n Dri packets to each diner. Place a lemon wedge alongside each individual casserole or on a separate serving dish. Serve this robust meal piping hot with thickly sliced sour dough bread as an accompaniment. Makes 6 generous servings.

 # CUYAMACA CLUB

I never knew, until recently, that the Cuyamaca (pronounced Kwee-a-mak-a) Club was the oldest private club in the state. When it started there were twenty-five members and that was the year 1887. Then, as now, the emphasis is on gracious dining midst handsome furnishings with impeccable service. In eighty-five years, although the Club has gone along with changing times, it has always maintained that original elegant but comfortable aura.

Presently the Terrace Room dining facilities occupy the top, or ninth, floor of a prestigious San Diego building. On another floor, the Men's Grille is a sanctuary for breakfast and lunch, offering the businessman extended hours to enjoy the fine food.

Come 1973, the Club will be expanding and transplanting its luxurious surroundings to a grand new building nearby, complete with handball and squash courts and spa facilities for men and women. As at the 1972 address, the dining room is on the top floor; but the new one will be more spacious with a fabulously designed, bigger and better kitchen to contain all Chef Constante Alcantara's dreams in equipment. Meanwhile, the Club manages quite well; and their adaptability and flexibility are the products of good management and a good staff.

And that's what I'd like to elaborate upon. My first

visit to the Cuyamaca was about seven years ago, when Ret./Rear Admiral R. Brevard Moore's wife, JoAnn, invited me. She and her husband frequented the Club so often and the employees are so constant, that she could rattle off waiters' and waitresses' names as if they were her southern cousins. At dessert time my imagination was piqued by the menu recommendation for *Strawberries Romanoff, Cuyamaca.* So for explanations she asked Bob Bowden to come over. He is the man who sets the metronome of the dining room in motion, the majordomo of Cuyamaca.

When I queried, "What's different from the usual Strawberries Romanoff?," he pointed out that he had acquired this recipe while traveling in Germany, and it was indeed different from French versions. He suggested I try it...I did, and I liked it.

Since then I have been there frequently, by day and night, in their private rooms, or as a member of a party taking over the Terrace Room and dancing under the stars. The roof of the Terrace Room slides open to reveal a magnificent sky, and that heavenly vastness seems to diminish the window views of non-smoggy San Diego from the Mexican border to the beach areas.

The Cuyamaca Club is older and wiser than most restaurants; theirs has always been a highly reputable dining room and club where experience shows. So since for many people happiness is a fine meal, and delightful surroundings make it even more pleasant, the coming years, during which the Cuyamaca will become a centenarian, should be the best yet for this grand old institution.

No menu at the Cuyamaca is without Chef Alcantara's gourmet specialty, Totuava (pronounced tutu-a-va), Mexican sea bass. And the way in which he prepares it is super deluxe: a lovely thin filet of fish rolled with a (shelled) King crab leg inside, sautéed to a golden brown and topped with Cuyamaca Sauce. Other filets of white fish may be substituted for the Mexican sea bass. But the Sauce is a must in anyone's recipe collection, for it makes an excellent dip with the Mexican vegetable, jicama, or with celery root or seafood.

TOTUAVA STUFFED WITH KING CRAB LEG

1 1/2 pounds thinly sliced (on a slant) filets of totuava
     (or white fish) cut in about 4'' squares (about 8 pieces)
About 8 pieces King crab legs or 1 package (6 ounces)
     frozen crabmeat, defrosted and drained
1 egg
2 tablespoons water
Flour
1/2 teaspoon salt
1/4 teaspoon pepper
2 tablespoons each butter and oil
Cuyamaca Sauce, see Index
Parsley

Place one crab leg or one or more tablespoons crabmeat on each piece of fish filet. Roll and secure with toothpicks as needed. Whip egg briskly in bowl with water; dip fish in briefly, then roll in mixture of flour, salt and pepper. Sauté in butter and oil over medium heat until banana color. When done remove fish rolls to warm platter and serve hot with Cuyamaca Sauce on top and parsley to garnish. Makes 4 ample servings.

Seafood Grotto

Earl's at the Wharf is perched just high enough to overlook the mundane and scan the action in San Diego harbor. For every diner there's a 180-degree view through circular glass walls...there are no bad tables. Occupying stage front and center in the panorama is San Diego's historic iron sailing vessel, the Star of India. Beyond are Navy and Coast Guard ships and itinerant boats plying the waters of the harbor at varying speeds.

It was this nonpareil scene that impressed owner Earl Gagosian and his wife Kay when, after completing the first five-story section of his Royal Inn Hotel, they checked in for the weekend and spent almost all of the next two days eyeing this marine spectacle. The life on the Wharf and on San Diego Bay was so fascinating that the following week Earl scrapped plans for a Royal Inn addition and got busy designing a restaurant which would afford diners the same pleasure, with gourmet seafood, of course!

Earl's idea of an unlimited view was combined architecturally with the shape of a convex shell...a giant mollusk to be exact. While the best shot of this man-made specimen can be seen from the adjacent Royal Inn towers, especially the details of the whorled motif and small off-center turret, some of the shell-like features are obvious from ground level.

Indoors has been decorated like an early conquistador's sailing ship with fine oak paneling, shields and emblems, and galleon copper lanterns, all in subdued tones of rust, burnt-orange and umber. Despite the tremendous exposure of glass the effect is softened and intimate.

Often lunch is gingerly treated, with a few hot entrées and several cold salads, but not at Earl's. Their menu encompasses fifty items. You'll find exotic dishes such as Fried Crab Claws, French Fried Lobster, Eastern Oyster Sandwiches, and Low Calorie Tuna Tug Sandwiches (a Tug happens to be a generous portion of tuna). Earl's philosophy for a proper seafood restaurant is a lot more than just fish and tartar sauce!

Chef Tony Cortez avoids short cuts, as he believes this renders seafood tasteless. "Fish are very delicate and require delicate preparation," says Tony, and this fact is evident in one of the dinner specialties he names for Mr. Gagosian, Earl's Crepes. You'll find it on the menu as Crepes de Fruits de Mer, which simply means thin pancakes stuffed with a variety of seafoods, coated with Hollandaise and broiled...*deliciously* delicate.

EARL'S CREPES

1 cup Hollandaise Sauce*, see Index

Crepes:
6 tablespoons flour
1/4 teaspoon salt
1/2 teaspoon baking powder
1 egg
1/3 cup milk
4 tablespoons water
Oil and butter

Sift flour with salt and baking powder in small bowl. Beat egg; beat again with milk and water until very frothy. Make a well in dry ingredients; pour liquids in, quickly beat together (ignore some lumps). Heat equal portions of oil and butter to grease a 5-inch skillet and place over medium heat. Pour about 2 1/2 tablespoonfuls batter in pan; tilt it to spread across bottom. Cook golden on one side, flip and cook lightly on other. As crepes are done, stack on warm plate. Re-oil skillet for each crepe. Makes about six or seven 5-inch crepes, enough for 3-4 servings.

Seafood Filling:
1/2 cup butter
4 shallots, diced
4 green onions, diced
4 small cloves garlic, minced
1 teaspoon cornstarch
1 teaspoon lemon juice
2 teaspoons Worcestershire sauce
2 teaspoons brandy
1/8 teaspoon monosodium glutamate
1/8 teaspoon pepper
1/2 teaspoon salt
1/2 teaspoon sugar
3/4 cup fresh or defrosted lobster meat, diced
3/4 cup fresh or defrosted shrimp, diced
3/4 cup fresh or defrosted crabmeat, diced

3/4 cup fresh or defrosted scallops, diced
3/4 cup cooked mushrooms, diced
Parsley to garnish

In a large skillet with butter, sauté vegetables until limp. Blend cornstarch with juice, Worcestershire and brandy. Add dry seasonings; pour into skillet and cook and stir with vegetables until thick and clear. Add seafood, sauté about 5 minutes; add mushrooms. Spoon seafood mixture on crepes; roll up loosely, place in rows on ovenproof platter, top with any remaining sauce. Place in preheated 350° oven for 5 minutes. Remove and cover crepes with previously prepared Hollandaise Sauce. Return to oven; broil to glaze top. Garnish with parsley. Makes 3 to 4 servings.

*Canned or bottled Hollandaise Sauce may be substituted here.

GOLDEN ROLLIN BELLY

I really would like to have seen the hilarious reaction down at city hall when the ficticious business name application for Golden Rollin Belly was filed. Perhaps the clerks are sufficiently saturated with kooky names not to bat an eyelash at one more, but, Golden Rollin Belly?

In case you wonder, the GRB restaurant name was lifted from the theme song of the entertainment group headed by Don Selby, one of the partners in the restaurant. If you still don't get the connection; shake hands.

I'll admit to having heard some odd names for pub-restaurants in the British Isles, Ireland, maybe even a few in New Zealand and Australia, but I think the Golden Rollin Belly deserves an accolade for being particularly unique.

Aside from the name, which is supposed to convey the idea of a merry old English pub, it looks just like a pub,

49

both outside and inside. The interior is a retreat to the Elizabethan period and the trimmings are all there; the rescued wooden beams (as distressed as the Bounty's), leaded windows (now having a resurgence of popularity in architectural design), balconies (right out of some Shakespearian drama, or is San Diego's Old Globe Theater missing any?), and trimmed church pews (straight out of Wuthering Heights.) To round out the scene there are comely serving wenches (like those in *Tom Jones.*)

Don Selby's partner in the GRB is the chef, Ernie Whellus. Ernie has some menu fillers that takes the GRB out of the steak and lobster-house class. Ernie also strives to carry out the "golden theme" (from the name), and the menu boasts Cheese Soup, Lemon and Ginger Salad Dressing, and chicken with a golden sauce. Your waitress announces the house specialty, a casserole which varies each night, but always goes well with their delicious dinners.

Come to think about it, someone once said, "An army travels on its belly." Do you suppose that is the connection? I know, when I leave the GRB I feel as though I have eaten enough for an army!

There are two good reasons for Crab Meat D'Jon, one an excuse to go to the GRB for this, their friendly Friday night house specialty, the other an excuse to prepare it at home because it's so quick and easy. From start to finish, it takes no more than fifteen minutes preparation time. Yet it is distinctive and a seafood you'll enjoy.

SAUTEED CRAB MEAT D'JON AU RIZ

1/4 pound butter (or 4 tablespoons each butter and oil)
6 medium mushrooms, sliced
3 green onions, finely chopped
1/8 teaspoon salt
1/4 teaspoon white pepper
1/4 teaspoon garlic powder
1 teaspoon monosodium glutamate
1 1/4 pound fresh or defrosted crab meat
1/3 cup (about 2 1/2 ounces) finely grated
　　Parmesan cheese

1/3 cup dry white wine
1 tablespoon fresh lemon juice
Steamed rice

In a large skillet over medium heat melt butter. Add mushrooms and simmer a few minutes; add onions and seasonings. Stir mixture well; simmer a few minutes. Vegetables should be just limp and not turning color. Add crab meat. Sprinkle cheese over all lavishly. Pour wine onto mixture. Gently stir to blend ingredients, trying not to create any stringy pieces. Simmer over low heat five minutes to reduce juices. Sprinkle lemon juice over ingredients before serving. Serve hot over steamed rice. Makes 4 ample servings.

La Casita

If you have been hoping to find that clean little restaurant with a broad menu, located conveniently in downtown Tijuana, La Casita (the little house) is your place. Hurry there before they expand, for although Bob and I enjoy the intimate ten table restaurant as it is, they do have expansion on their minds. After all, who wants to turn away business?

Their menu is a bit of everything, there's no way you couldn't find your mood food on it. What's more, the German chef, "imported" from Mexico City, has embellished the standard continental and Mexican selections with some French, Swiss, Italian and even Greek dishes that are truly noteworthy.

La Casita is Mr. Bejarano's pride and joy. His experience in the restaurant business came through his affiliation with Caesar's in Tijuana. When he decided to branch out on his own, he trained his two sons, Lito and Fernando, to help him with the guests; now the trio plus one (the chef) does such a whizz bang job that there is serious talk about enlarging.

La Casita is typical of Tijuana decor, black leather with red table cloths; and you can depend on good food and service in a friendly place. The produce and meats are all purchased in San Diego to provide American guests with the same quality they might find in the better restaurants on their side of the border. So it's a moot question. If it grows, will La Casita still be the little house that its regular customers dote on, or will the change be drastic ...necessitating food economy, non-family service, an unhappy hurried chef, and no time for the pleasantries that the Bejarano family provides? It may become spacious and able to accommodate more people, but...

For now it's handy, cozy and friendly, and right where you'd least expect to find this choice spot in Tijuana. But it's not touristy, so look for it.

Here's a different and delicious seafood dish. It's almost a fondue, but it isn't; and it's almost a curry, but without the curry ingredients. What it is is a distinctive way to prepare shrimp. If you like either cheese fondue or shrimp in most cooking styles, this is a natural...an exquisite combination!

CAMARONES A LA SUIZA
(Shrimp Swiss Style)

1/2 cup dry white wine
1 pound Switzerland Swiss cheese, cubed or grated
1 can (5 1/3 ounces) evaporated milk
Salt and pepper to taste
12 slices bacon, cut in small pieces
3 tablespoons each oil and butter
About 1 1/2 pounds (18-20) large shrimp, peeled, cleaned
*   and deveined*
1/4 to 1/2 cup sour cream
Steamed white rice to serve four
1 jar (2 ounces) sliced pimiento

In a medium saucepan over medium heat bring wine to

boil. Add cheese; stir constantly until melted and blended. Continue to stir to avoid sticking to pan bottom, and lower heat. Add milk; season to taste. Mixture should be very thick and stringy; set aside. In a large skillet over medium heat sauté bacon until crisp. Remove bacon and drain on paper toweling. In same skillet, over same temperature, heat oil and butter. When butter is melted and foamy, place shrimp in pan to sauté to pink on both sides (about 2 minutes each side). Turn and sauté three more minutes before removing from heat. Scrape skillet, pouring shrimp with butter juices into saucepan containing cheese. Reheat, stirring over medium heat. When piping hot stir in 2 or more tablespoons of sour cream to thin mixture to a heavy sauce consistency. On each plate place a serving of prepared hot rice. Pour over each a good portion of shrimp and sauce. Garnish tops with dollops of sour cream; add pimiento, then sprinkle bacon bits. Makes 4 servings.

Soon after we moved to San Diego, friends steered us to Lubach's. From that moment on we've been steady customers. Lubach's is no Johnny-come-lately; there is a feeling of dependability about it. And a splendid blend of big city ambience with a small town seaport's outlook. Situated on Harbor Drive, Lubach's is a one-story red and white frame building with a washed-ashore fishing boat in the front yard. Inside, the boat theme becomes more sophisticated with finely built boat models displayed against paneled mahogany walls above intimate, tufted leather booths. At one end the room is cheered with a glowing fireplace, and at the other you are welcomed with an inviting salad bar and grill.

It's a place to meet friends and to be greeted and fawned upon by the familiar faces of their unchanging staff. Moreover, Lubach's consistency in fine food and service has earned them six years of *Holiday* Magazine Awards. To put it succinctly, Lubach's is everything you'd like a restaurant to be.

Mr. R.C.A. Lubach Sr., a native of the Netherlands, and his son Bob have instilled continental traditions in their restaurant, and under their constant supervision "it works." Their cuisine is real...no short cuts. Smoked salmon, sliced ever so shear, is as good or better than any in the world. Their way with local *totuava* (Mexican bass) is a delight; and although the desserts are not touted as "special" on the menu, in my book they rate comment. Lubach's still makes their own Cheese Cake and a Parisian-style yeast-raised Baba au Rhum...both top-flight.

Lubach's is as popular by day for business men's luncheons as it is nightly for party groups or romantic dinners. It also appeals to San Diegans of all ages. Recently we dined there to quietly celebrate our thirty-third anniversary. We thought we'd come a long, long way together until we heard another couple in the adjoining booth toasting theirs. Like us, they were Lubach's "regulars," but in upmanship they were one-up on us...it was their fiftieth!

Lubach's is not solely a seafood restaurant, but when they do prepare fish or shellfish it's done very well. One of the more exotic dishes on their menu is Shrimp Cabrillo, a charcoal broiled specialty. It's a great idea for home barbecuing, or to do on electrical rotisserie skewers if you have that sort of appliance. This recipe is like Shish Kebab, but with fast cooking shrimp replacing meat on the skewers. Shrimp Cabrillo is served with a Spanish accent of bright red saucy sauce...olé!

SHRIMP CABRILLO
24 extra large shrimp (about 10 to 12 per pound)
1/4 pound sliced bacon, cut in 1-inch pieces
2 bell peppers, cut in 1-inch squares
18 large fresh mushroom caps
Vegetable or olive oil
Melted butter
Cabrillo Sauce, see Index
Parsley sprigs
Lemon wedges

Peel, clean and devein shrimp. Prepare bacon and peppers; rinse and trim mushrooms. Rub oil on shrimp. On skewers thread 1 shrimp, a piece of bacon, a piece of pepper, 1 mushroom and repeat, ending with a shrimp. This amount of ingredients fills about 6 (standard size) rotisserie skewers.

Prepare Cabrillo Sauce and let simmer while broiling shrimp. Broil shrimp over charcoal about 8 minutes on each side, or 15 minutes on a rotisserie. Shrimp should turn a nice pink, peppers slightly olive and mushrooms brown. Remove from fire; remove ingredients from skewers to warm pan or platter with melted butter on the bottom, and keep warm. Allow about 4 to 6 shrimp per person and serve with sauce on the side. Garnish plate with parsley and lemon wedges. Steamed rice and a green salad are good accompaniments. Makes 4 servings.

Bahia* MERCEDES ROOM

A car buff would be absolutely enchanted with the theme of the dining room and cocktail lounge at the Bahia Hotel, for it's almost a Mercedes-Benz Museum. From the foyer, where a meticulously polished and spot-lighted antique Mercedes car is shown, on to the hall, where the machinery "works" are presented in a glass enclosure, and then to the inner areas where the "art decorations" consist of attractively mounted and properly glistening car parts, these "basic black" rooms are similar to shadow boxes as they display fine technology in a gem-like way.

If your interest isn't strictly cars, you can focus your attention on the bay view window wall and watch the water sports. In fact, the dining room is stair-stepped, theater style, to afford all diners a good view of the action of bathers, boaters, or people boarding the old paddle-wheel boat, the Bahia Belle. On some occasion before dinner you might enjoy a Bahia Belle cruise around the Mission Bay waters, with cocktails and dancing as the sun sets. It may sound touristy, but speaking for the author and friends, even San Diegans find this a good pace-changer for an evening out.

Return to the smart, sophisticated atmosphere of the Mercedes Room, where the flexible menu lets you suit yourself. Unlike it's namesake, the car, the prices are not up there; yet the choices range from the Chef's special, Corned Beef and Cabbage, to Gourmet Breast of Capon "Cordon Bleu," or from Lox and Cream Cheese to Oysters Rockefeller. After all, this room does bear an enduring, proud name; and, in the food business, as in cars, consistent performance in all areas is what counts!

A "fair and warmer" weather favorite of mine is the Seabreeze Salad. Since it's composed of seafood and greens, it seems appropriately named for this bayside hotel and restaurant. To be a bit different, Chef Alfonso includes tuna in his recipe, which, besides being a tasty addition, is a reminder that San Diego is home port for those beautiful purse-seiners (ships) of the United States tuna fleet.

SEABREEZE SALAD

8 large decorative lettuce leaves
1/2 head lettuce, shredded
1 cup cooked lobster meat

1 *cup cooked crab meat*
8 *large cooked shrimp*
4 *medium tomatoes*
2/3 *cup drained canned tuna*
1/4 *cup diced celery, optional*
Mayonnaise or sandwich spread
     for mixing tuna and celery
Mayonnaise for garnish
8 *pitted black olives, halved*
2 *hard-cooked eggs*
4 *lemon wedges*
8 *white asparagus spears*
8 *anchovy filets*
8 *pitted green olives, halved*
1 *cup thousand island dressing*

Arrange large lettuce leaves on individual plates, placing shredded lettuce in center as bed for other ingredients. Slice lobster in 1/2-inch thick slices; arrange around outside edge as a ring. Shred crab, or leave chunky, and place in ring inside lobster ring. Butterfly large shrimp by splitting down back; place in scalloped style inside crab ring. (Rings of ingredients become smaller working toward center of plate). Quarter tomatoes, leaving bottom connected; scoop out centers. Mix tuna with celery and mayonnaise, or simply sandwich spread. Stuff tomatoes with tuna salad. Set each tomato inside shrimp ring and top with a dollop of mayonnaise and black olives. Garnish each salad with remaining ingredients, except for dressing. Serve salads chilled, with separate thousand island dressing. Makes 4 generous servings.

ℛℬ RANCHO BERNARDO INN

History happened here, and as one enjoys the thoroughly modern conveniences combined with the architecture and ambience of a Spanish ranchero it's good to contemplate, momentarily, life then and now. Rancho Bernardo land was originally explored by Spanish conquistadors, later settled by Mission padres, fought over by Mexican Californios and federal troops, and finally became several cattle ranches. If you had your druthers, wouldn't you prefer the present improvements of this particular era to the sport of life during those historical times? Or is it a moot question?

I, for one, prefer the air of the past in design, and the advantages of the present in food and services. I'm a sissy when it comes to roughing it and readily admit to enjoying the luxuries of today. The Inn at Rancho Bernardo is a resort with excellent dining room facilities. It caters to vacationers or people who visit there as an experience in gourmet dining. It offers a wide variety of eating arrangements, in various rooms. El Bizcocho, the Fondita and the Grandee suit the whims of just about anyone.

If you can dream up a scheme for up to twenty-four people to meet and eat in the Grandee Room, you will have a real moment to remember. This is the gourmet dining room where it isn't unusual for between six and fourteen courses (with a separate wine for each) to be scheduled for the Inn's guests. In the Grandee, French Chef Escoffier's gourmet rules are followed by The Inn's Chef Manfred Hacker, and that means the recommendation that no alcoholic beverages except wine to be served and no smoking allowed before or during meals, in order to keep the palate as pert as possible for the extra special meal. Prices start at $25.00 per person, but as I said, dining at the Inn is an experience.

The Chef makes the dining moments memorable whichever restaurant you select. By birth an Austrian, he has been just about everywhere during his lifetime. He learned his trade as an apprentice to a "crazy German chef," who also schooled him in the almost lost art of sculpting center pieces from basic kitchen staples. He absorbed the culinary arts so well that he wound up as Chef for Great Britain's Queen Elizabeth for two years, and proudly holds a letter of reference from Her Highness. And while working at Avignon Frères in Washington, D.C., he served President John F. Kennedy. Maestro Hacker is a great artist in his field.

On second thought, history is of great interest, to read about and to know where it happened, but even though the crinolines of this period were very becoming and the heroics of the times very invigorating...I'll still take what's here and now. I like the look of The Inn, the resort atmosphere, the truly elegant menus, the service, and I'll pass up all the "High Noon" dramas with guns or swords that used to take place on these grounds.

To achieve a true bouillabaisse, you may have to trek to Nice or Marseilles; but our Southern California seafood is a passing fair duplicate with Chef Manfred Hacker's recipe. Thackeray, often quoted on the subject, says he never could decide whether bouillabaisse is "a soup or broth, or brew, or hodge-podge." To me, it is all those things at once; the Frenchman's cioppino. A very hearty dish that's good fun to eat.

BOUILLABAISSE

3 tablespoons olive oil
1/2 large onion, finely chopped
1 clove garlic, minced or crushed
1 large leek, finely chopped
2 tablespoons finely chopped parsley
2 tomatoes, peeled and chopped
1 cup clam juice
1 cup dry white wine
2 cups water
2 tablespoons tomato paste

2 teaspoons salt
Pepper to taste
1 pound halibut (or other white fish), cut in 1-inch pieces
12 medium size raw shrimp, cleaned but with shells
6 scrubbed clams
6 scrubbed and debearded mussels or
6 to 12 scallops, optional
1 whole cooked lobster, cut up with shell
French bread, garlic seasoned, optional

Over medium heat and in a deep pot heat olive oil. Sauté onions, garlic and leek until limp. Add other ingredients except seafood. Cover pot and simmer fifteen minutes. Add uncooked seafood; simmer ten minutes longer. Add cooked lobster with shell to pot; heat five minutes with other seafood and stock. Serve in bowls with large portions of garlic-buttered French bread or toast placed in bowls before Bouillabaisse is dished into each serving, or serve garlic bread on the side. Provide a discard bowl for shells and bones and supply an abundance of paper napkins. For total enjoyment this dish should be eaten with a bib on. Makes 4 servings.

Shelter Island's
Bali Hai

Mitchener's Bali Hai was a verdant, jagged mountain island floating somewhere in the South Pacific, unapproachable and tantalizing. It was rumored that the feasts and entertainment there were beyond belief, but unfortunately intangible. In San Diego it's different. Bali Hai is at one end of Shelter Island, set apart but very accessible, and the feasting and entertainment are worth all your efforts to swim, boat, walk or drive to reach it. If it's a tropical mood you desire, follow the palms and ferns into the exotic world of tiki gods, tapa cloth and flickering candle-lit lanterns and hurricane lamps...all the comforts of a deluxe Shelter Island restaurant with the nuances of fictionalized Bali Hai.

Cocktails are served in the South Pacific Room, which occupies the first floor of Bali Hai's Samoan-designed restaurant. Here, too, is the place for Polynesian-style fun. Nightly (except Monday) there's a wildly exotic floor show with sword and fire dancing as well as the more traditional Polynesian entertainment. There's even music for your own dancing, which, after a Whaler's Punch or Tahitian Manhattan, you just might be in the mood for.

The pièce de résistance is the food and the view from the Top of the Isle Room. For getting down to the serious business of dining, this roundtop room satisfies the discriminating palate and offers a panorama of San Diego Harbor waters from the north end. Yachts come and go, and some even dock at a barely visible pier just below... and there's always the rising San Diego skyline with about the same remoteness as Bali Hai to an accessible South Pacific island.

The food and service are outstanding, from puu puus (Polynesian appetizers) on through the usual and the unusual South Pacific entrées. From the wide assortment one may choose Oyster Filet of Beef, Lobster à la Fong or Chicken of the Gods, to name but a few. It's best to have your waitress clue you in on what goes best with what for a variety of flavors to suit your party. Less adventurous folk will appreciate the excellent Prime Ribs of Beef.

For a romantic experience, reading Mitchener's *South Pacific,* with its fabled Bali Hai, is hard to beat; unless you compare it with dining at this beautiful, for real spot on Shelter Island.

It's hard to pick favorites when everything seems "best," but for a distinctive Cantonese dish that Bob and I enjoy again and again, it's Chicken of the Gods. This dish is not the usual soy-sauced Chinese or Polynesian combination of foods; in fact, the only way I can express it is "light, delicate and heavenly."

61

CHICKEN OF THE GODS

1 (2 1/2 to 3 pounds) uncooked chicken, boned
Bones, neck and giblets removed from chicken
6 cups water
1 egg, beaten
1 tablespoon dry sherry wine
1 teaspoon soy sauce (light preferred)
1/4 teaspoon salt
Dash of white pepper
1/2 pound water chestnut flour
* or 1 cup cake flour*
1/4 cup oil
4 tablespoons butter
1/2 cup all purpose flour
2 tablespoons cornstarch
1 cup cream
Salt and pepper to taste
1 canned chicken broth, if necessary
1 tablespoon toasted sesame seeds

Add water to pot containing bones, neck and giblets. Bring it to a boil; cover and simmer for one hour. Strain and drain liquid, discard bones and reserve stock. Marinate boned chicken pieces in mixture of egg, wine, soy sauce and seasoning for 15 to 20 minutes. Coat each piece with water chestnut or cake flour. Sauté chicken in oil in skillet over medium heat. In a medium saucepan melt butter, blend in flour and cornstarch. In another pot reheat and bring to a boil one quart of the chicken stock. Pour the stock by the cupful into the butter mixture, stirring rapidly, over medium heat. When blended and mixture boils, reduce heat but continue to stir occasionally. When mixture is very thick, add cream and seasoning; do not boil again. Sauce should be a heavy consistency, but if too thick add canned chicken broth to achieve proper thickness. Cut chicken pieces in neat slices and arrange attractively on heated platter. Cover with cream sauce. Sprinkle sesame seeds over the top. Makes 3 servings as a single entrée.

Jim Hom's CHINA LAND CAFE

Don't expect glamour, magnificent furnishings or more Orient than Occident when you visit Jim Hom's China Land Cafe. Jim Hom's main claim to popularity is not so much what intrigues the eye, but what pleases the palate. Further, they offer crackerjack service and super-convenience in location. China Land is only about one-half block from the Midway Drive-Rosecrans Boulevard intersection; and since the construction nearby of the San Diego Sports Arena (a mere two and one-half blocks away), the recreation-minded have found it an ideal spot for odd-hour meals before or after events at the Arena and elsewhere.

For many nearby localites China Land is right on the way home, and because it's a drive-in as well as a restaurant, it's a great stopping-off place for food on the run or to enjoy at a table, time permitting. Your choice of foods may be either Chinese or American; and both are created by chefs, not machines. Jim Hom is the manager of this twenty-two-year-old going concern; backing him up is a regular United Nations staff working to prepare the kind of food and give the kind of service he knows the public wants. And they do.

During the time I was writing a food column in the San Diego *Union,* a reader wrote to ask for help in obtaining a recipe from Jim Hom's. It wasn't for a particularly uncommon Cantonese dish; for many Chinese restaurants offer a version of Got Let Chicken. But her request was for *their* recipe, since she felt it was superior to others. Needless to say, as a newcomer in the area I was personally interested and anxious to learn more about the recipe myself. In English, Got Let Chicken means Chicken Wings in Red Sweet-Sour Sauce, and I found it made an equally delicious appetizer or family-style dinner main course.

FOWL & GAME

So often a person yearns for different tastes, but can't see bothering to cook or hasn't the time to do so. If that's your problem, Jim Hom's is the place to go for service "on wheels" or specially prepared food. Drive-ins are pretty run of the mill, but not Jim Hom's. In this computerized, pre-packaged, pre-cooked world it's good to know that at China Land *people* are still involved.

Chicken wings seem to be a waste of time as they are, but with a little Chinese imagination and a bit of dexterity these inexpensive pieces can become the Cinderellas of your table. As small drumsticks, they are deep-fried then covered with a savory red sauce and sesame seeds. When you serve them, introduce them by name and you'll be speaking a little Chinese.

GOT LET CHICKEN
Chicken Wings
2 pounds chicken wings
1/2 teaspoon monosodium glutamate
1 1/2 teaspoon salt
1 cup flour
1/8 teaspoon pepper
1/4 cup cornstarch
1 egg
1 cup water
2 tablespoons oil
Oil for deep-frying
Red Sweet-Sour Sauce, see Index
1 1/2 teaspoons toasted sesame seeds

First, check with butcher; sometimes he has "drumettes" ready. If so, the following procedure is unnecessary. Using regular wings, chop off wing tip at first joint; discard tips or save for soup stock. Cut wing at next joint and remove two thin middle bones, but leave meat from this section hanging onto remaining large bone (the one that resembles a drumstick). Pull this meat inside out over large end. With a small knife, scrape and push all meat to

64

end, forming a round of meat like a drumstick; do this to all wings. Rub each wing with a mixture of monosodium glutamate and 1/2 teaspoon salt. Combine 1/2 cup flour, 1/2 teaspoon salt and the pepper in a paper bag. Shake chicken in bag. In one bowl combine remaining 1/2 cup flour, cornstarch and remaining 1/2 teaspoon salt. In smaller bowl beat egg lightly, add water and oil to it. Blend together in bowl with dry mixture to make batter. Dip floured chicken in batter and fry in deep fat or oil heated to 400° in electric skillet or large skillet with deep fat thermometer, until golden brown. Drain on paper toweling. Keep chicken warm in 150° oven until all pieces are fried, or up to 1 hour (before serving). Reheat previously prepared Red Sweet-Sour Sauce, but do so slowly. Serve wings warm with sauce on the side as an appetizer or poured over wings on a platter as a main course. If sauce is poured over, garnish top with toasted sesame seeds. Makes 3 to 4 servings as one of several main courses; much more as an appetizer.

La Fenière

If the restaurant itself has merit, location really isn't all that important. La Fenière (an old French word derived from *fenil,* meaning silo or barn) is proof in point. Picture a group of stores on a main commercial street; put a TV repair shop on one side and a Frosty Freeze on the other, finish off the scene by sandwiching a French restaurant in between these shops . . . and there you have La Fenière.

If it crossed your mind to ask why one should name a perfectly nice French restaurant "The Barn" (especially when it's not even in the country), I assure you there is no obvious connection. The subtle reason is because the owner, Atif Kriem, has happy memories of a French converted barn restaurant by the name of La Fenière in his home, Rabat, Morocco. So now he has created an unbarn-

67

like restaurant in San Diego, It's sort of interesting to think that Rabat, Morocco, and Pacific Beach, California, U.S.A. share a restaurant name as a common denominator. More so, to learn that three San Diegan families have been to La Fenière in Rabat and then sought out the Kriem restaurant because of it!

Atif Kriem is a handsome, exotic-looking young man and, although this is his first experience owning a restaurant, he has distinguished himself in other areas. Atif came to Louisiana from French Morocco as a member of the Peace Corps to teach French; then he moved to Washington, D.C., and switched to Arabic instruction. Later Atif moved to New Orleans, which was about as French in ambience as you could get in the States. Atif finished his doctorate and then the University of San Diego came up with a full-time job for Atif teaching French.

So you may wonder why he opened La Fenière. Well, it followed naturally. He missed the New Orleans nightlife and excellent restaurants; he had a yearning for a typical, small and intimate place with good food and service. Hence, La Fenière. He contributes menu items from his family's recipe collection and the menu is limited but ever changing. By offering only five entrée selections at a time, La Fenière has a better shot at quality control. While alternating the dishes every so often keeps the steady customers happy, for they have the opportunity to savor "new" French delicacies.

Dr. Atif Kriem may have no past history in the restaurant game, but he seems to know the essential ingredients for winning. His "street cafe" restaurant is not out to gain architectural or interior design awards, (although it is scheduled for redecoration) but the food is certain to please . . . and what could be more important? As we Americans might put it, that young Kriem has started out on the right foot. He should make it here in San Diego County.

Because of the method of preparation and the combination of the zesty flavor of duckling, this is an absolutely delightful French dish. If you despise this fatty bird or find it offers a scarcity of meat, forget all of that. The fat is skimmed away, and my suggestion is you make two ducks so there will be plenty to go around. Or you'll wish you had!

CANETON AUX OLIVES
Duck with Olives

1 (about 4 pounds) duckling
Salt and pepper, to taste
2 tablespoons oil
1 onoin, finely chopped
1 carrot, finely chopped
1/3 teaspoon thyme
2 bay leaves
6 parsley sprigs, chopped
2 tablespoons butter
Approximately 24 large ripe green olives
1 teaspoon salt in water to cover olives
3/4 cup chicken stock, or canned broth
1 tablespoon lemon juice
Freshly ground pepper
Parsley

Sprinkle duckling with seasoning. Heat oil in large casserole or dutch oven over medium high heat on range; place duckling in pot and brown on all sides. Prepare bouquet garni, composed of thyme, bay leaves and parsley. When duckling is lightly browned all around remove it to a platter; drain liquid from casserole. Place butter in casserole over medium heat and melt it; add onions, carrots and bouquet garni. When vegetables have become limp, place duckling on top; cover casserole securely and bake in a preheated 350° oven for one to one and a half hours. Prepare olives by heating over medium heat in saucepan with salted water to cover; simmer 5 minutes, and drain. When duckling is tender, remove it to a platter, strain vegetables and discard, but reserve liquid. Skim some of grease away; return duckling to braising juices of casserole; arrange olives around it. Add chicken stock to casserole (liquid should almost cover the olives). Cover the casserole and return it to the oven for about 20 minutes. Skim off as much fat as you can, when duckling is done. Season the juices with lemon juice and fresh ground pepper gratings, if desired. Serve duckling on platter with olives around it and garnish with parsley. Pour sauce over or serve in sauce or gravy dish. Makes 2 to 3 servings.

Mi Burro

Have you ever wanted to eat at a sidewalk cafe, yet not wanted to be engulfed by clouds of dust or insects? If so, go to Cantina Mi Burro. You *can* have this delightful outdoorsiness and still be indoors, unbothered.

Mi Burro is colorful and gay; it has a decor typical of a sidewalk cafe or a Mexican garden. There are myriad pots of enormous bright paper flowers, festive *piñatas* here and there, beautiful *serapes* on the walls, even awnings to complete the setting. The *serapes* are really worth looking at twice, for they're extremely handsome and very old. These weavings were done by the Aztec Indians and depict scenes of their life style.

There's a good view, too, across Harbor Drive to the San Diego Wharf and today's only floating iron clipper ship, the Star of India. Visit this museum ship before you lunch or dine, then when you've worked up an appetite, Mi Burro has a treat in store for you. Their recipe *especial* is for Margarita fanciers; this beverage, made from Mexican Tequila, is oh-so-smooth, and served by the pitcherful! But, since sobriety is a requisite for negotiating the narrow treads down into the Star of India, it's best to sightsee first, then enjoy the pleasure of the Margaritas.

Mi Burro's food is Sonoran style, simply delicious, and not highly seasoned. It's great for a change in eating patterns. There are separate rooms for large parties or family get-togethers; and best of all, the price is right.

My husband, Bob, prefers the Sonora Steak Picado (marinated pieces of filet), but I strongly boost the delicate Mi Burro House Special (Sour Cream Chicken Enchiladas). We both agree the Chile Con Queso and Guacamole Dips are marvelous for chasing the Margaritas, or vice versa! There's good Mexican house wine by the glass or the litre and Carta Blanca, the numero uno of Mexican Beers. Try Mi Burro, You'll *like* it!

If you're not familiar with making Mexican dishes, don't panic. This is quite easy to prepare, and you'll be glad you did. The Sour Cream Sauce is one of those lovely recipes that serves more than one purpose: use it as an appetizer dip with tostados (corn chips), then another time make the enchiladas. They are *muy especial.*

SOUR CREAM CHICKEN ENCHILADAS

2 cups (1/2 of 2 1/2 pound fryer)
    cooked chicken, cut into strips
2 tablespoons each oil and butter
1/2 tablespoons each oil and butter
1/2 small onion, chopped
1/2 bell pepper, chopped
1 fresh tomato, diced
1/4 cup water
1 1/2 tablespoons flour
3/4 cup chicken broth
1/2 teaspoon salt
6 (8-inch) or 10 (6-inch) corn tortillas
Oil or shortening for frying
Sour Cream Sauce, see Index

Cut chicken into small strips; set aside. In skillet containing oil and butter, sauté onion until limp; add pepper, cook a few minutes more, then add tomato. Mix water and flour until smooth; blend mixture into chicken broth. Add broth to vegetables; simmer and stir until thickened. Season with salt; stir in chicken. Set aside; preheat oven to 450°. Soften tortillas by sautéing (one at a time) in hot shortening over medium-high temperature in medium-sized skillet. Cook each tortilla a few minutes on both sides; turn and remove with a pancake turner. Place tortillas in large baking dish. Spoon about two or more tablespoons (according to size of tortilla) of filling over each tortilla. Roll, and now they are enchiladas. Place each enchilada close together in baking dish. Prepare Sour Cream Sauce. Pour sauce over enchiladas, covering them completely. Put baking dish in oven and bake 15 minutes. Makes 3 to 4 servings of 2 or more enchiladas per person.

PUCCI'S Villa Fontana

The newest of the Ramada Inns, which San Diegans knew before as the Villa Fontana, has retained all of the good features of the original Mediterranean-style hotel. Situated somewhat loftily on the south side of Hotel Circle in Mission Valley, this hotel of Moorish-Spanish architecture needs only a sparkling blue sea beneath to make you believe you're on the Costa Brava. Pucci's is the restaurant that culminates this dreamy impression. Tucked away as it is in the center of the hotel, deliberately dark and romantic in its continuity of the Spanish theme, Pucci's is intended for intimate dining. Like the setting of the fountain garden, also in the midst of the hotel, Pucci's is a place of quiet, away from worldly chaos.

Drive up, park your car, stroll through the door and leave your cares outside...they'll keep. It's easy to forget as you scan the extensive menu. There are so many good French or Italian, or Chef-inspired dishes to choose from that a return visit may be a necessity. Each time we have lunched or dined at Pucci's I've pondered the menu like a kid in a candy store. All is good, but which should I have? It always results in another visit.

If you find yourself in a luncheon "rut," try Pucci's Frittata di Spinaci (a 3-egg omelette with Italian sausage, spinach and mozzarella cheese); it's a substantial enough meal to tide you over until dinner. Often it's such a struggle to think of something different for the mid-day meal...but Pucci's has the answers. Their dinner menu is more elaborate, and includes many foreign dishes that take time for preparation; it's a good idea to order those specialties with your reservation. For example, how many places serve pheasant baked in clay?

To illustrate the remarkable sort of culinary experiences that Pucci's offers, why not try the clay-baked bird at home? Of course, the first trick is finding a small pheasant...but don't be deterred, a rock cornish game hen will do nicely. For easier preparation, I skip the boning procedure. The second stopper might be the clay...but don't give up on that, simply visit an artist's supply store for some plain gray pottery clay. (It's especially prepared for kitchen use and is moist and ready to use.) Then don't forget to pick up some prosciutto ham, wild rice, truffles and Madeira wine when you shop for the birds; for these are unlikely items to have on hand. Believe it or not, when this conglomeration is put together in the prescribed manner you'll not only have fun in the making and serving of it, but will find the results outstanding.

FAGIANA A LA CRETA
Pheasant baked in clay

4 cups boiling water
1 teaspoon salt
1 cup wild rice
1 can (2 ounces) sliced mushrooms
4 boneless baby pheasants or
    4 boneless rock cornish game hens
Salt and pepper to taste
1/4 cup softened butter
Paprika
1/2 pound sliced prosciutto ham

10 pounds pottery clay
2 cups Madeira Wine Sauce, see Index

Prepare wild rice: Rinse well, drain, stir into salted boiling water. Cook without stirring about 40 minutes. Water should evaporate; if not, drain. Add mushrooms. Remove giblets from birds; season inside with salt and pepper. Stuff with wild rice-mushroom dressing. Rub birds with softened butter; season with salt and pepper and sprinkle lavishly with paprika. Wrap birds with prosciutto slices; wrap again in square of aluminum foil and carefully seal openings. Divide clay into 4 pieces; roll out, like pie dough, into 10-inch squares. Place birds in center; mold clay around bird and shape like a flat-bottomed football. Place birds on baking sheet in preheated 300° oven; bake 15 minutes. Increase heat to 350°; continue baking a minimum of 1 hour and 30 minutes. Prepare Madeira Sauce while birds are baking. To serve, crack clay with small hammer in kitchen, or if you have been creative and have sculpted a design, serve in clay at the table. Unwrap foil and carefully remove bird. Add any natural juices in foil to Madeira sauce. Serve each bird individually with accompanying sauce; garnish with spring vegetables. Makes 4 servings.

Atlantis

The architect who dreamed up Atlantis Restaurant must have had Debussy's *Sunken Cathedral* for his music to draw by, for it has an elegant, from another world and space look to it. The mood he has created has the imaginative concept of the famed lost continent for which it was named. Built almost on a level with the Mission Bay water that partially surrounds it, it conveys the effect of arriving on a temporal land mass that one day will disappear from sight altogether, into the depths.

Myth-making in human culture has been part of the

lore we have shared with past generations and will continue to do so with those to come. Atlantis is a favored spot in lost continent mythology; a mighty nation, land of philosopher kings and brave warriors, sometimes referred to as the Isles of the Blest or the Fortunate Islands.

That's it; that describes this Atlantis. As you step "ashore," here is all the best of science fiction writing, philosophic theories and poetry spelled out in rock and stone, with understated landscaping and decorations that blend yet don't offend. Instead of meeting an Atlantean, possibly a twelve foot, three-eyed creature like those said to exist on some supposedly sunken continents, you'll find an attractive hostess who will seat you at a secluded booth or table, or time permitting, usher you into the fantasy-filled cocktail area, where the wall behind the bar is a giant aquarium. It's a romantic, utopian sort of atmosphere, and if at once you're not convinced you are somewhere else, take time. Look out the huge plate glass windows past the tropical foliage edging the buildings and waters, and gaze across the Bay to the shimmering lights of the land known to brother humans as San Diego.

When you arrive at menu selections you'll find an agreeable combination to choose from. There are Polynesian pupus and Mexican antijitos (snacks) and then sea food, poultry and meats done in a variety of earth styles. My palate is most pleased with the spinach salad and the Veal Mediterranea.

So, if this isn't Lemuria (between India and Africa), nor Mu (in the Central Pacific), and not Islandia or the true Atlantis (both in the Atlantic), I must be dreaming. If so, please do not disturb.

Spicy, yet delicate; this is a truly innovative recipe of Executive Chef Nick Recio's. It's the sort you can come away from wanting more, and should you indulge you won't have that uncomfortable sensation. Whether you sail across the seas to Atlantis or whip it up in your own kitchen; you'll start believing in mythology.

VEAL MEDITERRANEA

Provençale Sauce, see Index
1 1/2 pounds veal cutlets
Seasoning salt and pepper, to taste
Flour
Mornay Sauce, see Index
2 avocados, peeled
2 tablespoons each butter and oil
1/2 cup heavy cream

Prepare Provençale Sauce; let simmer about one-half hour or until reduced to pulpy consistency. Pound (tenderize) veal with cleaver or meat hammer. Trim fat from meat; cut into serving portions. Sprinkle with seasoning; cut into serving portions. Sprinkle with seasoning; coat with flour. Let meat stand on wax paper. Prepare Mornay Sauce; cover and let stand. Slice avocadoes in half, then cut lengthwise (removing seed) in 8 or 10 pieces; leave ready to use on wax paper. Sauté veal in large skillet in butter and oil combination. When done remove to warm bake and serve platter. Whip cream. Quickly pour Provençale Sauce over meat. Decorate meat slices on platter with avocado slices. Fold whipped cream into Mornay Sauce and pour over meat, covering platter to the edges. Place platter about four inches from broiler and glaze sauce to a golden color. Serve immediately. Makes 4 to 6 servings.

There's more to Tijuana than the main drag of Avenida Revolucion. Follow the cars out to the Aqua Caliente Race Track area and you'll see another face of this city. Part of the interest in that direction now is restaurants. Granted, the track is no more, because of fire, but there's still the golf course and across the street from it an Italian restaurant that's worth your investigation.

Boccaccio's, as this restaurant is now known, really started in 1927 in downtown Tijuana. It was not Boccaccio's then as the first owner, Arturo Provenghi, named his restaurant after his wife, Marianna. When Carlos Boccaccio took it over a year later he renamed it Boccaccio's Nuevo Marianna (New Marianna.)

Twelve years later Carlos retired. His younger brother, Domenico, after working with Carlos since his arrival from Bari, Italy two years previously, took over the business. For the Boccaccios, whether here or in Bari (which is at the heel of Italy's boot), restaurants have been the family trade. Judging from the excellent foods served in Boccaccio's in Tijuana, their reputation is well established in this hemisphere.

In 1957 Boccaccio's Nuevo Marianna went up in smoke and it took awhile to recoup the family's losses, but by summer of 1960 there was a Boccaccio's still newer Nuevo Marianna on Boulevard Aqua Caliente. The location was great for golfers and track fans, as it was convenient to the golf course and the race track. Then the Aqua Caliente Race Track also went up in smoke. Traffic on the boulevard slowed down tremendously...but, for those of us who like to avoid crowds, that made it nicer. Now the visitors who go out Aqua Caliente way have golf or food on their minds and Boccaccio's will always be a fine attraction. It is a restaurant of international cuisine with emphasis on Italian specialties. The bar is well stocked, and the wine display, like the food menu, is international and impressive.

But the best of Boccaccio's is the family tradition that keeps this restaurant abloom. Nowadays you will be greeted by Mrs. Boccaccio and her two sons, Francisco Antonio and Domenico. They will make you welcome in their warm manner and help you choose from the menu according to your taste. With an international flavor, their selection ranges from baby octopus to Saltimbocca (veal cutlet) and the pasta is super.

It's true...there's a lot more in Tijuana than meets the

eye. Some places, apt to be the best in town, are easily missed, unless you are in the know...such a place is Boccaccio's.

The name Saltimbocca, which literally means jump in the mouth in the Italian language, doesn't explain what are or how to make these meat morsels. Boccaccio's Saltimbocca is a veal steak rolled with proscuitto and mozzarella cheese inside, sautéed and topped with Fiorentina Sauce, a most delicious fresh mushroom concoction. Who knows...maybe this Saltimbocca could jump in the mouth!

SALTIMBOCCA ALLA FIORENTINA
Veal rolls with Fiorentina Sauce

Fiorentina Sauce, see Index
1 1/2 pounds veal round steak, cut in (2-ounce) slices
8 paper thin slices prosciutto ham
1/4 pound sliced (about 8 pieces) mozzarella cheese
Salt and pepper to taste
Flour
About 3 tablespoons olive oil for frying

Prepare Fiorentina Sauce and set aside. Tenderize veal cutlets with meat hammer or cleaver. On top of each cutlet or medallion of veal equally distribute prosciutto slices and then cheese. Roll veal, wrapping it over ham and cheese. Secure each roll with toothpicks. Season to taste and sprinkle with or roll in flour. Heat olive oil in large skillet over medium temperature. Sauté veal rolls until each is light brown. Remove to heated platter. Drain grease from skillet; pour prepared Fiorentina Sauce into skillet. Reheat quickly over medium high temperature. When bubbling, pour over Saltimboccas; serve immediately. Fettuccine al Triplice Burro and romaine salad or a variety of cooked vegetables go beautifully with Saltimbocca. Makes 4 servings.

CAROUSEL
Vacation Village

Vacation Village is simultaneously a state of mind and a San Diego destination point. It is the heart of a forty-three acre island known as Vacation Isle, and although easily accessible it seems remote, being entirely surrounded by the waters of Mission Bay.

No high-rise project this; "V.V." is built in luxurious single story cottage clusters complete with individual patios. Privacy and relaxation, sports and entertainment are all possible in this escapist's paradise. Yet across the causeway from this palm-dotted island is San Diego's world famous Sea World, an all day experience, while in the opposite direction you can leap into the big breakers of Pacific Ocean beaches. A bit farther south lies another San Diego "world famous," the Zoo, and old Mexico is scarcely more than a half hour away. "V.V." is a dream come true for getting away from it all...but with creature comforts.

You can have your cake and eat it too at "V.V."; do as much or as little as you desire. You can be aloof or gregarious. And when it comes to thoughts of food, drink and entertainment, don't think there isn't an all-out effort to please. You can be just as informal as you wish at the Barefoot Bar and Jack's Steak House, or you can slip into some slippers and tie on a tie and go after the brass ring. Where? At the nearby Carousel on the grounds. Everything desirable in the way of drink and food can be found in the cocktail lounge or restaurant which is an integral part of this resort hotel. Kiosk-like in structure, but so sizeable it is almost a round Samoan-type meeting house, it has South Pacific wave lengths that emanate from the use of abundant foliage, Tiki gods, cork floats and nettings. Furthermore, there's been much artistic effort put forth in the unusual use of two-by-fours, tele-

79

phone poles, shingles, brickwork and steel reinforcing rods! Amazing, yet so effective.

Don't ask me how this restaurant of pseudo South Pacific ambience came to be called the Carousel. My answer might imply some relation to the international merry-go-round selection of foods. It's as if all you need to do is catch the brass ring for a fleeting food trip. You name it, they have it at the Carousel.

It's a nice thing, when choosing a restaurant, to know of one that can cope with varied appetites and tastes. I say, "Stop the Carousel, I want to get off...this is my kind of place!"

Here's a recipe for Sauerbraten at its best. My husband's favorite food is done to a turn with the Carousel's formula. It is pot roast with a gentle twang.

SAUERBRATEN

2 1/2 to 3 pounds beef bottom round
1 1/4 cups red wine vinegar
1 1/2 cups water
3/4 cup dry red wine
3 bay leaves
3 cloves garlic, sliced
1 teaspoon black peppercorns
1/2 teaspoon (whole) thyme leaves
1/2 cup sugar
3 tablespoons oil or shortening
1/4 cup butter
1/4 cup flour

Place meat in deep crock or glass bowl. Combine vinegar, water, wine, seasonings and sugar; pour over meat. Cover and marinate in refrigerator for three days. Liquid should cover meat more than half-way; turn meat daily and recover. After three days, pour marinade from meat, reserving liquid. Brown meat in oil or shortening. Pour one half marinade liquid over meat; reserve other half. Simmer covered, as a pot roast, for two to three hours until tender. Turn meat several times during cooking period. In a saucepan, over medium heat, melt butter and stir in flour making a thick roux. Strain reserved marinade into butter-flour mixture. Stir and cook until thickened. Remove tender beef to warm platter. Strain beef juices-marinade into thickened sauce. Slice beef for serving. Serve with red cabbage and potato pancakes, as at the Carousel; or as we like it, with sauerkraut and potato dumplings. But don't plan on left-overs regardless of what accompanies this dish; there probably won't be any. Makes 4 servings.

Elario's

In La Jolla, which seems to be the eatingest place in San Diego County, there's a prime new dining spot, Elario's Restaurant. It's on the Inn-Top, which is the eleventh floor of the plush Summer House Inn. The room has a sweeping view of the shores from Alligator Point to Scripps Oceanography Institute. And at this height, the sunsets can be eyed on a level as they slowly, then rapidly, slip beneath their nighttime comforters.

Albert Frettoloso is the attractive manager of Elario's and he comes with top credits from no less than San Diego's Kona Kai Club, Mr. A's and Pucci's. If you don't already know him, you'll quickly see he has the savoir faire for Elario's fine continental cuisine restaurant.

You may have wondered what cloud up there around the eleventh floor was tapped for the name of the restaurant; for after all, who ever heard of a restaurant named Elario's? Exactly...but in this case it happens to be Albert Frettoloso's father's name. And, if you think about it, "Elario's" is different, a bit musical, and definitely expresses the continental theme.

Chef Ernie Contreras gave the kitchen its shakedown cruise April 15th, and in that immaculate, mechanized,

MEATS

last-word-in-equipment kitchen he proved his own metal. Even though Chef Ernie's kitchen was a whole new world to work in, he produced a tremendous diversity of dishes. As any housewife who has moved about frequently knows, getting used to new stoves, ovens, dishwashers or what- ever else she's blessed with is like learning arithmetic fractions all over again. It's not much easier for the pros. Still, it came off well and we are pleased to include this prestigious restaurant to La Jolla's ever-growing rostrum.

Besides it isn't every day you can enjoy lunch or dinner with La Jolla's Soledad Mountain on one side and it's Riviera coves and rolling seashore on the other. It's hard to beat the green and blue tones of hills, sky and water from this lofty loge. These days almost every city can boast of restaurants on top of downtown skyscrapers. But from there what can you see?... only the city! This view is different. From Elario's restaurant on the top of the Summer House Inn, you have the feeling it's always sum- mer there, and that's nice.

Sooner or later I'm sure you'll try all of Elario's spe- cialties, but for a tempting at home selection, why not treat your loved ones to their recipe for veal cutlets? It's simple, yet looks and tastes as though much T.L.C. has been given to the preparation. Besides, if you can man- age the Italian name, you'll impress your loved ones even more.

VEAL CUTLETS ALLA BOLOGNESE: PAPPAGALLO

1 egg
2 tablespoons water
6 (3 to 4 ounces) veal cutlets
2/3 cup bread crumbs
1/3 cup grated Parmesan cheese
1/2 teaspoon salt
Pepper to taste
3 tablespoons each oil & butter

6 slices boiled ham (cut to fit veal)
1 cup milk
1 cup canned tomato sauce
1/2 cup dry white wine
1 teaspoon Romano cheese

Whip egg with water until foamy. Dip cutlets into egg mixture; remove and dip into combination of bread crumbs, 3 tablespoons Parmesan cheese and seasoning. Reserve remaining cheese. Let meat set on wax paper 15 minutes before cooking. Sauté cutlets in large skillet in hot oil and butter over medium heat about 5 minutes on each side. After turning once, top pieces of veal with ham slices. Combine milk and tomato sauce with wine and pour over cutlets. Cover pan and simmer for about 25 minutes. Place meat on warm serving platter and sprinkle Romano cheese over all. Makes 4 generous servings.

Fontainebleau

The Westgate Plaza

To many people Fontainebleau recalls a French town, or an extensive forest or a favorite palace of French kings; but in San Diego it has another significance. Here it relates to one of the most lavishly decorated dining rooms in the world; one that serves gourmet food comparable to the best.

Envision the Fontainebleau restaurant as a crown jewel mounted in an elaborate antique setting. Its surroundings are so elegant they seem to substantiate the regality of the gem itself. In truth, this extraordinary restaurant is situated in the heart of what *Esquire* magazine has selected as "one of the three greatest hotels in the world," San Diego's fabulous new Westgate Plaza.

The public rooms, tastefully decorated in the styles of Louis XVth and Louis XVIth, are authentic to the last detail. The paintings, tapestries, sculpture, Persian carpets, hand-cut crystal chandeliers (four men are em-

85

ployed full-time keeping them immaculate), magnificent antique furnishings and the unique collection of art treasurers are all veritable museum pieces. The completeness and perfection of selection belies description. Come to think of it, the Westgate Plaza would make a very handsome residence for either of the Louis's, were he living here today. Though he might lift a brow at our conveniences, snuff at our politics, and most certainly would have to levy new taxation to pay for this extravagant $14.5 million palace...it it were his.

Throughout the Westgate, the power behind the thrown is more than evident. You can sense a woman's touch, for there is charm, warmth and thoughtfulness in myriad little things as well as in major works. Helen Alvarez Smith, a petite brunette dynamo, was the decorator extraordinaire; her efforts are a tribute to harmony in the entirety. And Dusty Clayton, titian-topped, industrious and whip to her co-workers, charms people with her nature and competence as the catering manager.

The broad and exciting menu of the Fontainebleau restaurant speaks for itself...it offers la crème de la crème ...and the skillful and innovative talents of Canadian-born Executive Chef Roger Jones are evident. He has been awarded the *Toque Noir* (black hat), a much envied prize for the highest achievement in culinary arts. So, even if you have reservations about some of the innovative dishes, I suggest you try them; you'll find many poetic masterpieces.

If you truly enjoy opulence, first look around at the brilliant chandeliers, damask cloths, gold rimmed china, fine crystal and oyster velvet chairs; then bear in mind that they are just the setting. The real jewels of the Fontainebleau are the meals themselves.

The dish Chef Roger and I have chosen for your enjoyment is one that you will probably back away from after looking over the list of ingredients. Must admit, I reacted in the same fashion; nevertheless, it's a rave recipe to our taste buds. If you're game; try this different, tarragon-flavored veal. The tarragon is delightfully emphasized by whiffs of anise-flavored Pernod and the result is...sublime.

LES MEDALLIONS DE VEAU VIEUX CARRE
Veal Medallions in the style of New Orleans "Old Quarter"

8 pieces (3-ounces each) veal tenderloin or cutlets
1 egg, beaten
2 tablespoons water
Flour
4 tablespoons each oil and butter
1/3 cup butter
1/3 cup tiny cooked bay shrimp
1/3 cup sliced fresh mushrooms
1 chopped shallot
1/3 cup Pernod
Tarragon Sauce Mousseline, see Index

Flatten veal pieces to scallopini thinness. Beat egg with water until fluffy. Dip veal pieces in egg and drain them; coat with flour. In a large skillet, sauté them quickly and gently in mixture of oil and butter over medium heat. Place sautéed veal on warm platter. Have topping ingredients ready: in medium size skillet over medium heat, sauté the mushrooms and shallots in butter. Add Pernod. Bring to a boil, add shrimp, and heat, but do not boil. Cover veal slices with this mixture; then cover all ingredients with Tarragon Sauce Mousseline and glaze under broiler, until golden. Makes 4 servings.

GRANT GRILL

Wow! One of man's last strongholds has yielded to our changing times and, ladies, we've lucked-in. For years and years, the Grant Grill was well-known among San Diegans as the one place women were truly unwelcome, until after 3:00 P.M. Men could conduct business, simply socialize, or do whatever it is they do for three glorious hours without the fuss of feminine distraction. But lately there have been some intrusions. Upon occasion, a women's libber would prance through carrying a placard for equality, but even she was rarely eye-balled by the masculine majority deep in heavy man talk.

Close to San Diego's center city, Grant Grill is ideal for the businessman or the man who deals with the local administrative offices. Now it is a great new spot for the housewife downtown shopping or the single girl on her lunch break. The Grill has always been crowded...even in "men only" days...but now, ladies, you, too, can join the crowd. And if you can't squeeze in the Grill, remember the Garden Room. It's more spacious and, if you're not entirely absorbed with the quick-meal-and-away idea, the chances of catching a man's eye there are just as good.

At dinner, the Grant Grill is still the place to go to see and be seen in San Diego. Travelers also respect the Grill and consider it to be a reputable restaurant with the charm of private dining in surroundings of quiet restraint. Booths and tables have been artfully placed to assure each its own share of intimacy. You may have to discreetly ask your waiter if that really was John Wayne sitting in the adjacent booth!

Most people carry away a nebulous feeling about the Grill, and if called upon to describe it may mention something about the decor...the elegance of the subdued reds, the mellowed wood paneling and the burnished leather, and that large mural of the landing of the explorer Juan Rodriguez Cabrillo; or the service of attentive but unobtrusive waiters; or fond memories of the savory turtle soup with sherry, or some of the other flawless time-tested recipes.

Recently the Grant Grill was expanded by the addition of the Cabrillo Room. This extra space accommodates individuals and groups up to forty, with the famous Grill menu and exceptional service still available. Cabrillo may have landed here, but the U. S. Grant Hotel and its Grill came to stay.

From the Grant Grill's widely varied menu of international entrées I've selected our favorite. It's a border town specialty which the Grill calls Tournedos Acapulco. If you enjoy carné asada (marinated, sautéed beef tenderloin) with a peppery flavor this might be your choice too.

TOURNEDOS ACAPULCO

Acapulco Sauce, see Index
1/2 cup butter
8 thinly sliced rings of green pepper
8 (1/8-inch) slices Bermuda onion
8 (3 to 4 ounce) beef tenderloin filets
Salt and pepper to taste

Melt butter in large skillet over medium heat. Sauté pepper and onion slices very lightly until just barely limp. Remove and set aside. Season beef slices and cook to degree of doneness preferred. Place beef on heated platter; top with an onion and pepper slice and Acapulco Sauce. Reheat a few moments in 400° hot oven. Makes 4 servings.

What's in a name? Where restaurants are concerned, it can entice you, or as easily wave you off with dullness. The importance of this must have crossed the minds of David Ronce, Dale Finney and Jim Christ (pronounced Crist) when they put their heads together and determined to build their place. To me, the concept of their entire restaurant is one of an artistic assemblage of bits and pieces of this and that, a montage. The name obviously had to have a germ of reference, but otherwise remain abstract. Notsom Flotsom means absolutely nothing, yet it intrigues.

However *flotsam* (spelled with an "a") does mean something. It refers to the floating parts of a ship's wreckage or the cargo from it; we might commonly call it *junk*. The play on words could be "not some flotsam," and as applied to their establishment, interpreted, not some (not any . . . more grammatical) flotsam (junk) restaurant . . . did I lose you? On another track, though the interior decor may at first appear to be a collection of oddities, never let it be said that there's a bunch of junk in this place, for it has all been carefully assembled. Whatever the basis for the name, it's proved to be a mind-bender for us; and I'll bet Bob and I are not the only ones!

To go back to the three young owners. There was one that liked to cook, another who preferred to paint, and a third who liked to manage and keep books. The artist in the trio collected old wooden office chairs that squeaked, as a hobby, and yearned for a place to paint his favorite cartoon characters. And so they all do what they like and know best in their own place, Notsom Flotsom. The result is utterly charming and disarming. The cook produces excellent food, geared to suit the steak and lobster trade, but he also has fun with a wacky salad bar. The unbelievable "bar" is a converted old-fashioned bath tub! This bulging antique is really quite nice and extremely attractive with over twenty fresh raw vegetables, plus sesame seeds, raisins, and croutons spread out for you to Dagwood your own salad.

The artist couldn't be happier than when there's a full house and everyone is relaxing in his squeaky old office chair. It sounds like a cricket convention. He has painted, on the walls, to his heart's content. There are mural size pictures of Dr. Seuss' characters and his other cartoon favorites, Yosemite Sam, Bugs Bunny, The Hulk, Dagwood, Aquaman, Mustard Man, Pogo, and Flakey Sloont.

Judging by the brisk business, I would guess the management end of the team is satisfied . . . as he laughs his way to the bank. You'll sense it, there's an informal, relaxed merriment expressed in the interior design and the general attitude. As for my reaction to the restaurant in total, I have to say, "It's not some flotsam kind of place."

This is a delicate marinade for extra special steaks that you don't want bowled over by a pungent teriyaki steak marinade. When you get the best in meat, as at Notsom Flotsom, you should be able to taste the beef and not drown it with seasonings.

RIBEYEYAKI STEAK MARINADE

1 pint dark soy sauce
1 1/2 cups hot water
2/3 cup organic alfalfa honey
   (other varieties may be substituted)
1 tablespoon sake or dry white wine
1 tablespoon cold-pressed safflower oil
1/2 teaspoon garlic powder
1/4 teaspoon ginger
4 (12 ounces each) ribeye steaks, or substitute Spencer,
   New York, porterhouse or T-bone cuts

Prepare marinade ahead of time, in order to cool it before marinating steaks; marinade should be room temperature when poured over beef. Put ingredients into large saucepan over medium heat and bring to boil. Stir occasionally. Let boil, then remove from heat. Cool fifteen minutes. Bottle, if storing (under canning procedures); if using immediately cool to lukewarm and pour over steaks in a convenient size baking dish (to let steaks be covered by liquid.) Let marinate for one half hour, then turn and continue to marinate for one hour. Lift steaks from marinade to oven or charcoal broiler. Strain and drain marinade into bottles and refrigerate for future use. Makes 1 1/2 pints sauce, which is ample for four steaks to serve four persons.

OLE OLE

After thirty years of success with quick sandwich type meals and mass service, Bill Fielder did an about face and chose a spot in Solana Beach where people would come because of unusual food, personalized service and camaraderie. No more "Hasty House" and "Snacks" Drive-in's where hamburger orders were taken, with simply the qualification of rare, medium or well. He bowed out of Fielder-Barry Inc., the parent company of Hasty House and Snacks Drive-in establishments in Kansas, Colorado, Oregon, Arizona and California when he decided to operate an intimate Mexican cuisine restaurant in Solana Beach.

And he climbed the last important mountain in the hamburger business, when he introduced America's anytime-of-day food to Zurich, Switzerland. It was an instant success and so was Bill's chain of Silbir Kugel (silver ball) Swiss restaurants that served the burgers. But that enterprise now continues without him. After eighteen years, Bill Fielder felt he had commuted long enough!

In 1969 Bill came to California. In the past he had looked longingly at various towns along San Diego's coastline. So he put his idea to live here and manage a Mexican restaurant to the test. That did it. He became indoctrinated with our easy way of life and the neither too hot or too cold climate, and what's more he became addicted to Mexican foods.

Now Bill and his wife, Bibs, have Olé Olé and one goal. His know-how in restaurant management and his wife's flair for decor teamed up with a chef who knows what he's about in the kitchen and a bartender who pours a friendly Margarita, or whatever, from 11:00 A.M. to 6:00 P.M. at the bargain price of fifty cents. Together they have put Olé Olé on the restaurant map.

It's a very informal restaurant. Simple, but effective. We're glad the Fielders came here to stay. And about their restaurant we say Olé Olé.

Chile Verde is a quick and easy way to serve pork. What's more you'll like it because the chiles give it such a different flavor, very unlike traditional pork recipes. Chile Verde is popular all over Mexico as a stew, but bear in mind it is not bland. Be prepared for it to be *un poquito caliente* (a little bit hot), and blame the chiles, if you must. This is one of the most requested dishes at Olé Olé.

CARNE DE PUERCO CON CHILE VERDE
Pork with Green Chile Sauce

2 pounds lean pork, cut in 2-inch x 1/2-inch strips
Pork fat or 3 tablespoons oil for frying
1 to 2 cloves garlic, crushed
1 teaspoon salt
Pepper to taste
1/2 large onion, chopped
1 can (1 pound) diced tomatoes or canned whole,
*   peeled tomatoes, cut up*
1 can (4 ounces) diced green chiles or canned whole
*   chiles chopped or cut in strips*

93

1/2 cup water
2 tablespoons flour

Brown meat in pork fat or oil in a large skillet over medium high temperature. Add garlic, seasonings and onion. Cook stirring until onion is limp. Drain grease from skillet. Add tomatoes and chiles; stir to mix. Pour water in jar or mixing cup, add flour, cover tightly and shake well. Strain flour mixture into skillet and stir to mix thoroughly. Continue stirring until slightly thickened. Cover skillet; turn to low heat. Simmer for 30 minutes. Remove from heat and serve with Spanish rice, refried beans, hot tortillas or other Mexican side dishes. This mixture of pork with green chile sauce can also be used as a tamale filling. Makes 4 ample servings.

"RENO"

What a delightful surprise Reno is. The Reno I'm talking about is not the city in Nevada, it's a restaurant in Tijuana. Beyond the name there's no other connection, not any pin ball machines, "slots," neon lights, floor shows or even the wild or the casual West.

Tijuana's Reno is quite unlike the sprawling, border town surrounding it. The restaurant is urbane and cosmopolitan with an air of Mexico City's best dining rooms. Perhaps the most surprising feature of Reno's is the feeling you have as you step inside. There's such a contrast from outside.

Given a little time, your eye can't miss the enormous chandelier in the main dining room. The artist who created it didn't just make an ordinary fixture to light up the room. It was done to order for the Reno, and because of its size, had to be made and assembled on the premises.

There's no way it could be transported and brought in through normal passageways. This six months labor of love still has another finishing touch coming to it. On the graceful gold leafed metal arms the artist has fixed delicately colored enamel flowers; they're so lifelike you may be tempted to touch them. These buds are the final steps of the chandelier project, and one of these days there will be tiny lights protruding from each of them.

Oil paintings done by Señor Revelez, a local artist, are a complementary selection of scenes of the French Renaissance. Also emphasizing the continental ambience are the tables set with sparkling white cloths, silver and a single red rose, and pale olive green velvet chairs pulled up around them.

In another dining area with a dance floor that glows with soft lights from below there is dancing. In the future, the father Pepe Ortiz and his son Jorge, who own the Reno, plan to add a large golden seashell as an orchestra platform.

The Reno has a scant amount of Mexican dishes on its menu, but those you do find are very good. Theirs is primarily a continental cuisine, and it is so well done that between the food, service and appearance of the Reno you'll have a hard time believing this is Tijuana.

You can't pass up this menu suggestion when it's available, because the ingredients make it so very special. It's continental and hardly what you'd expect at a border town restaurant, but this is a select selection at Reno's.

TOURNEDOS A LA ROSSINI

4 slices dry French bread
6 tablespoons butter
4 center slices of filet mignon,
  (each about 1 1/2 inches thick)
2 tablespoons oil
2 tablespoons Madeira wine

1 cup Brown Sauce or canned beef gravy
1 teaspoon crumbled bay leaves
1 tablespoon brandy
4 slices pâté de fois gras

Prepare French bread by buttering with about 4 tablespoons butter. Sauté bread quickly over medium heat in large skillet, remove to platter covered with paper toweling. Sauté filets in oil and remaining butter in same large skillet over medium high heat, about 5 minutes per side for rare steak. At preferred doneness, remove filets to warm platter and keep warm. Deglaze skillet with wine and Brown Sauce (or gravy); add bay leaves. Let sauce come to boil, remove from heat and add brandy. Place slice of fois gras on toasted slice of bread. Top with filet then pour the sauce over the tournedo.
Makes 4 servings.

 **SARRETT HOUSE**

Shirley Sarrett intended her Sarrett House to be a fun place from the start: to attract non-stuffy people to sit at tables under suspended stuffed heads of moose, elk, buffalo and other game creatures. As a lark, her first menus offered mainly buffalo, prepared as buffalo burgers, stews, chili, steaks and stroganoff. And if buffalo didn't turn you on, there was always turkey, beef, pork ribs or salmon as alternatives. The menu was simple and all went well, except unintentionally Shirley sent the buffalo business skyrocketing. Prices zoomed and scarcity, as well as insecurity of delivery, gave her a few migraines. The result, new menus have cut back on the Sarrett House specialty, buffalo, even though these unseemly beasts apparently have a good toe hold along the La Jolla coastal "range."

And should you happen to be a lucky hunter and have a successful excursion, but not know how to prepare the wild game you've shot, Sarrett House will cook it to a turn. They have a way with game meat.

If you're curious how taste buds react to buffalo meat, Shirley tells me that only chili seasoning really diminishes the zesty flavor of the buffalo meat. I've had the stroganoff and it's much like the stew: they both exude a bit of the game smack. But buffalo steak is where the rich gusto is evident. For best bets though, the buffalo burger is a real winner; and it will be an occasional (whenever available) feature on Shirley's new menu at noon and night. It is sauced with a delicious barbecue-type sauce, one of her own good recipes (and there are many).

Besides having a successful dining room, attractive in its simple, high-ceiling, amber-lit, club-like decor the Sarrett House has the kind of bartenders you like to talk to; and Red Shade, who plays old time banjo in the lounge. It's a downright friendly place to visit.

If you can corner Shirley, when she's not riding herd or trouble-shooting on her range, or subbing for the hostess or bussing for the waiters, she has an amazing success story to tell. It begins awhile back with her arrival in "little" La Jolla, a place she once visited. From that point, with two babies and thirty-five dollars as her sole assets, she became a beautician. She eventually bought her own shop, and having successfully launched "The Hair Works," turned her talents to the Sarrett House and became a restaurateur! On that note I will bow out, singing "They wouldn't believe me"... but it's true.

Even if the buffalo don't ride your range tonight, don't worry, other meats work out just fine with this handy recipe from Sarrett House. It has a sauce that can be used with roasted or barbecued meats, spare-ribs, beef-ribs, hot doggies or whatever. If any sauce is left over, don't hesitate to use it as a French dressing of the sweet-sour sort...or make it from the beginning as such.

BUFFALO BURGERS

1 pound ground buffalo meat or beef
1/2 cup minced onions, optional
1 egg, beaten, optional
Seasoning salt to taste
1 tablespoon each butter and oil (optional)
8 slices bread or 4 split hamburger buns
Butter, optional
1/2 recipe Bar-B-Q Sauce, see Index

Mix meat with onions, and egg, if desired (the egg acts as a binder); add seasoning salt. Shape into patties about 3/4 inch thick. Grill over charcoal, in which case egg is a good additive as meat juices drip away into the coals; or sauté in skillet with butter and oil to preferred doneness. Toast one side of bread or bun; butter bread or bun, if desired, on untoasted side. Place finished patties on untoasted side of one piece of bread. Serve burgers open-faced or covered. Burgers may also be served without bread. Bar-B-Q Sauce may be poured over burgers or passed at the table in a sauce bowl. Makes 4 servings.

Schnitzelbank

For about as long as I care to remember, there's been a Schnitzelbank in La Jolla...and it's always been popular. Summer visitors, many of them devoted Del Mar Race Track fans, unfailingly found their way to familiar, favored places, and the Schnitzelbank was always one of them. I know I can't remember making a visit to the San Diego area that I didn't wangle a lunch or dinner at this quaint restaurant. In early days La Jolla was not known for its many eating spots, as it is now. What was there was seasonal and highly specialized. If you arrived out of season, you could expect to see closed signs. If you desired variety, this was not the place. So from away back the Schnitzelbank always intrigued me. It was one of the few places you could take the family without embarrassment, and the menu was good and very homey. A nice combination.

Evenings there were cozy and gemütlich. Schnitzelbank was designed in and out in quasi German style, similar to a small restaurant in a small town in Deutschland. It was family-oriented, and we usually arrived with our five children and sometimes their guests; as time passed we've had grandchildren in tow. We liked the change of routine home menus to those featuring Sauerbraten, Wienerschnitzel, Hassenfeffer and Goulash, and these foods seemed so much better when eaten with German wine and beer. The homemade pastry was mighty hard to pass up, but sometimes, when struck with indecision over the Apfelstrudel, I'd have Viennese coffee with whipped cream. Either way I'd have to rationalize on the calorie count; but how often could you enjoy such irresistible goodies? Best of all, we always departed secure that next year the Schnitzelbank would be just the same. It would never be ploughed under by "progress."

Thank goodness I can still report that the Schnitzelbank is alive and well and doing a brisk business all year 'round. Basically it's the same old-fashioned German domestic dining room with papa's and mama's chairs, and tables large enough to suit any size family. Their pewter and china collections and dark period paintings of earlier generations are for show and for sale. Owner Rudy Kloeble (from Ulm, Germany) is always there to welcome you. In fact, it's all there as Rudy Kloeble has kept it that way. Schnitzelbank is a foreign atmosphere for fun and food within the borders of the U.S.A.

To most Americans, goulash is a bad word, implying a pathetic mess. In Europe, however, goulash is relished as a hearty soup-stew and makes a great lunch or dinner dish. Nothing hits the spot better on a cool day, and aside from all that it's very nourishing. The Schnitzelbank's recipe has a flavor of caraway in the broth. After tasting their version, I wouldn't have it any other way.

GOULASH

3 medium onions, finely chopped
2 tablespoons each of butter and oil
1 pound lean beef stew meat, cubed
2 tablespoons flour
2 teaspoons salt
1 cup tomato purée
1 tablespoon paprika
1 teaspoon caraway seeds, optional
1 teaspoon dry marjoram leaves
1 quart water

In a heavy saucepan or Dutch oven, sauté onions in butter and oil over medium heat until limp. Add meat and brown lightly. Sprinkle flour over meat and onions and stir through to blend. Add remaining ingredients, stir to mix. Bring to a boil; reduce heat to simmer and cover pan. Simmer over low heat for at least one and one-half hours; cook longer if necessary for tenderness of meat. Serve piping hot in soup bowls with a hard roll or French bread on the side. If there are any leftovers, you'll find, as I have, it tastes better the second time around. Makes 3 to 4 servings depending on the type of appetites, whether it's for lunch or dinner, and if other foods are to be served.

 TEN DOWNING

There's something about visiting Ten Downing Street, San Diego, that makes you feel disoriented, as Alice must have felt in following the white rabbit. It's easy enough; you begin by walking a short but dimly lit passageway, which leads you to a hole-in-the-wall entrance, and from there it's down a few stairs, and lo...you've arrived. It's a strange sensation to be transported out of the heart of San Diego into a realistic, refined old English eating and drinking establishment, yet it's no dream. The room is complete with fireplace, fine quality round tables, high wingback, upholstered chairs, and even pretty wenches with English accents, costumed à la Moll Flanders.

In the daytime, local P.R. and ad people get away from it all here in order to take a break in an imaginative atmosphere, away from their own creative thinking. By night it's a place to dine as in one's own home, with fine period piece furnishings and the utmost in privacy in either the comfortable wing chairs or intimate booths.

The menu is cleverly drafted in the style of an issue of *The Illustrated London News* from the 1880's. If you care to pass some time reading before thinking about what to eat, you can learn a bit of shady English history from it, such as how the real No. 10 Downing came to be...through the nefarious maneuvers of one George Downing. If it's food you're interested in, each dish has been named for a one-time occupant of No. 10 or another British historical personality. Don't pass up the Northumberland Bread Soup, or the Tournedos of Beef Henry IV, and the absolutely beautiful Trifle...described on the menu as "England's Magnificent Understatement." And should you happen to be dining on a Monday or Tuesday night, Ten Downing gambles with the stock market and the cost of the closing Dow Jones Industrial Average! For example, if the Dow closes at 935, dinner for two is only $9.35, with your own menu selections. With an investment like this, how can you lose?

Maybe this is Alice's Wonderland after all. It certainly gives one pause to look around; so what better spot to slowly sup and talk of sealing wax and "cabbages and kings?"

One of the nicest things that can happen to a piece of prime filet mignon is to be turned into tournedos. In the case of Tournedos of Beef Henry IV, a generous portion of filet is split in half, sautéed, and placed on rounds of crisped bread, then the steak is dressed in a brown sauce and finally garnished with artichoke bottoms and topped with Béarnaise sauce. Add a few garden vegetables, a good wine and you have a dinner fit for the ruler of a kingdom *or* of your home.

TOURNEDOS OF BEEF HENRY IV

4 (7 ounces each) beef tenderloin filets
8 whole frozen or canned artichoke bottoms
8 slices dry white bread
4 tablespoons butter
4 tablespoons oil
1 can (10 1/2 ounces) Brown Sauce or gravy
1 jar (4 ounces) Béarnaise Sauce (or home-made)

Trim filets of all fat; slice each filet crosswise in half to make two 3 1/2 ounce tournedos. Cook frozen artichokes according to package directions or drain canned artichokes, and reserve for garnish. With a very large cookie cutter, trim bread into rounds; if no cutter is available, take your best aim with a knife and carve a circle from each slice. Spread each side of bread croutons with butter and sauté the pieces over medium heat in a large skillet; reserve on paper toweling for later use. Heat oil in same large skillet over medium high temperature. Sear and sauté filets to your choice of doneness. Pour brown sauce into pan, let it heat with meat a few moments, until it begins to simmer, then remove pan from heat. Place two bread croutons on each of four heated plates, top with two filet halves, pour on some Brown Sauce. Garnish top of steak with prepared artichoke bottoms and a dollop of Béarnaise Sauce on each artichoke. Serve with potatoes and green vegetables, or as you wish. Makes 4 ample servings.

San Diego has another new island called Harbor; and at the western tip of it a new Coast Guard beacon is housed, quite uniquely, in a restaurant. This beacon is unmanned and flashes automatically at five second intervals on a twenty-four hour schedule. Tom Ham's Lighthouse Restaurant, however, is anything but mechanized and has special operating hours. And rightly so, for it serves the public in a very different way. Tom Ham provides entertainment with cocktails on the main floor, and above there's a quiet, view-tiful cocktail area called 'Tween Decks, and a grand room for dining with fantastic vistas of San Diego's skyline, the bridge to Coronado and the Harbor.

The new beacon at Tom Ham's restaurant is an exact replica of the old Point Loma Cabrillo Lighthouse tower, fifty-five foot cupola and all. Together, with the early California architecture of the restaurant, it is a becoming companion piece. On the inside of Tom's restaurant there is a veritable maritime museum blended with a combination of Spanish and New England decor, circa 1880. From about 1845 on, the Yankee whaling fleet used to put into San Diego Harbor seasonally to prepare whale oil. Those were also the days of the hide trade, with San Diego the roundup point for cattle herding all the way down the coast from Sonoma. The *vaqueros* (cowboys) and the Indians slaughtered the cattle at the missions, then most of the meat was jerked (cut into strips, pickled and dried), and from 25,000 to 50,000 hides would fill a trading ship, eventually finding their use as New Englander's shoes. San Diego Harbor did a bustling business with seamen and they've always been greeted with open arms here.

Tom Ham's artifacts are mostly from the era of the

103

square-masted whalers and traders, with nautical items of all sorts that he has traveled the seven seas to collect. He even has an exhibit of scrimshaw, the carvings (from whale teeth and bones) that sailors used to do to pass idle hours of solitude on the vast, rolling sea.

As in bygone times when San Diego welcomed seamen to its shores, now there's a new beacon and restaurant that offers seafarers and landlubbers a new dining experience. At Tom Ham's Lighthouse, San Diego's high-living era is recreated and you'll be treated to a fare-thee-well.

Carné Asada (marinated, sautéed slices of beef tenderloin) is prepared in many different ways, but Tom Ham's method is pretty consistent and one that is particularly delectable to us. The *Salsa Fresca* (fresh tomato, vegetable sauce) topping also has many variations, and some recipes delete the cilantro, which, although typically Mexican, finds disfavor with some people. I suggest you substitute parsley, if in doubt. The Guacamole (avocado garnish) is an excellent recipe, and I've adopted it for my own use as an occasional salad or chip dip.

CARNE ASADA

2 to 3 pounds beef tenderloin filets (2 ounces each)

Marinade:
2 cups vegetable oil
1 cup soy sauce
Juice of 1 lemon
2 teaspoons cracked black pepper
1 teaspoon salt
1 teaspoon garlic powder
1 teaspoon ground oregano
1 teaspoon monosodium glutamate
Oil for frying meat
1 cup tomato juice
Salsa Fresca, see Index
Guacamole Supreme, see Index.

Lay approximately 16 to 18 cuts of beef filets on cutting or bread board, cover them with a clean cloth and pound lightly with meat cleaver. Combine marinade ingredients in large bowl. Place meat in marinade making sure marinade covers it well. Let stand approximately one hour. Remove meat; drain and strain marinade into jars for refrigerator storage. It may be used again. Pre-heat oil in large skillet; quickly sauté beef (two minutes). Add tomato juices; when it begins simmering remove meat from heat. Place meat and pan juices on platter and top with *Salsa Fresca.* Serve with Spanish rice and Guacamole Supreme. Makes 4 to 6 servings.

LA COSTA

It's like a spa, and you can diet La Costa style or follow a special physician's orders, but don't expect to see only people with problems. For La Costa is much more than a spa; it has a wide range of facilities for every age bracket and interest: golf courses to challenge daddys and mommys, swimming, horseback riding and tennis to particularly tempt the juniors. So you might say La Costa is more like a big country club, with extras.

What extras? Well, for starters, most country clubs don't have hotel accommodations ranging from rooms to full sized homes...but adding this feature to other assets would only make La Costa a delightful resort. And there are a lot of resorts. There are lavish and luxurious opportunities offered by the "personal program" where you can work towards thinning or thickening your body, go for beauty care and instruction or for classes of water exercise, yoga or isometrics; but these would make La Costa seem mainly like a spa. And there are a lot of spas.

On the other hand, food is everyone's concern. The pleasure or sacrifice of it can be the most important thing anyone does. La Costa covers the span from gourmet foods to rigid or specific diets. Now that's what makes it special, something more than a country club, resort or spa.

The main dining room overlooks the 18 hole championship golf course where the annual P.G.A. Tournament of Champions is held. I've visited for the opening night celebration, fashion show luncheons and private dinners. Whatever the occasion, the food prepared under Executive Chef Willy Hauser's anxious eye is always splendid. However, I feel that often the biggest challenge to a chef or cook is having to prepare rigid dietary meals (I've been the route!). For that reason I've selected a delectable menu from La Costa's Spa Luncheon, conceived for weight watchers. You can be sure that if Chef Hauser masters these fine dishes while having to count calories, what he turns out with no holds barred is superb.

LA COSTA SPA LUNCHEON
(284 calories per person)
Broiled Sherried Grapefruit (40)
Cucumbers Vinaigrette (16)
Braised Chicken Chasseur (146)
Fresh Carrots with Fine Herbs (36)
Peach Parfair (46)

BROILED SHERRIED GRAPEFRUIT

2 large table grapefruit, halved, centers removed
   and sectioned
About 1/4 cup dry sherry wine

Place prepared grapefruit halves on broiler tray. Sprinkle grapefruit generously with sherry. Place in oven about 4 inches from broiler; broil until edges of grapefruit turn dark brown. Makes 4 servings of 40 calories each.

CUCUMBERS VINAIGRETTE

1 large cucumber, peeled and thinly sliced
Water
1 tablespoon lemon juice
1/2 recipe Vinaigrette Sauce, see Index

Prepare cucumber by soaking one hour in bowl with about one cup or more of water and lemon juice, enough liquid to cover slices. Prepare Vinaigrette sauce. Squeeze ...drain all liquid from cucumber. Pour Vinaigrette sauce over cucumber slices in bowl. Cover dish with plastic or foil and refrigerate one hour. Makes 4 servings of 16 calories each.

BRAISED CHICKEN CHASSEUR

1 (2 1/2 pound chicken, cut in quarters, or selected pieces
    of the same weight)
White pepper
1/2 onion, finely chopped
2 medium tomatoes, peeled and finely chopped
1/2 pound fresh mushrooms, finely chopped
1 clove garlic, minced or crushed
1 cup (about 1/2 14 oz. bottle) dietetic ketchup
1/2 cup dry white wine
2 green onion tops, finely chopped

Preheat oven to 450°. Sprinkle chicken pieces liberally with pepper. Place chicken in bake and serve dish. Set on a middle rack of oven and roast at 450° for 30 minutes. Chicken should be golden and some juices should have accumulated. If completely fat-free food is desired, drain the juices from pan at this time. Combine onion, tomatoes, mushrooms and garlic and distribute over chicken. Combine ketchup and wine and pour over all. Reduce oven temperature to 325° and return chicken to bake slowly for 30 more minutes. Chicken should be tender to touch and done. If not, allow more time. Remove from oven,

107

scatter green onions over top. Serve piping hot. Makes
4 servings of 146 calories each.

FRESH CARROTS WITH FINE HERBS

1 2/3 cups fresh carrots, peeled and crossed-sliced
1 can (10 1/2 ounces) defatted chicken broth or stock
1 teaspoon finely chopped fresh or freeze-dried parsley
1 teaspoon finely chopped fresh or freeze-dried chives
1 tablespoon finely chopped fresh dill or 1 teaspoon dried
    dill weed

Prepare carrots. Pour chicken broth in small saucepan
over medium heat; add carrots slowly when broth is boiling. Boil until carrots are slightly al dente (firm) about
12-15 minutes. Drain stock (reserve for other uses such
as soup, if desired), add finely chopped herbs. Serve very
hot. This vegetable portion of La Costa's Spa Luncheon
contains 36 calories per portion. Makes 4 servings.

PEACH PARFAIT

1 can (16 ounces) artificially sweetened low-cal peach
    halves, undrained
1 teaspoon unflavored gelatine
1/4 teaspoon rum flavoring
3/4 teaspoon vanilla extract
1 teaspoon grated lemon rind
Few drops lemon juice
About 2/3 teaspoon of diet liquid sweetener or
    1/2 teaspoon diet powdered sweetener*
1 drop yellow food coloring, optional
Diet whipped cream, optional (adds 14 more calories)

Drain peaches, reserve liquid (there should be a little
more than 1/2 cup) and dice peaches; set peaches aside.
Pour reserved liquid into measuring cup and sprinkle
gelatine over it. Let stand 5 minutes; if gelatine has not
been absorbed, stir until blended. Place cup with gelatine

mixture in it into pot with hot water measuring half-way up side of cup. Heat slowly on stove over low heat. When gelatine has dissolved, remove cup. Cool slightly; add flavorings, rind, juice, liquid or powdered sweetener as desired and food coloring. Mix together, then pour over diced peaches. Check for desired dweetness. Pour mixture into dessert or parfait glasses. Refrigerate approximately four hours. Serve as is, or with a dollop of diet whipped cream if desired. Makes 4 servings of 46 calories each.

*Note: 1/2 teaspoon diet liquid sweetener = 1 teaspoon sugar. 1/10 teaspoon diet powdered sweetener = 1 teaspoon sugar.

RANCHO LA PUERTA

How long has it been since you flew a kite or have swung in a hammock? No matter when it was...you should...it's the kind of therapy everyone needs in this mod world. Living is complicated and fast; we need to get uncomplicated and function in slow motion; or we'll self-destruct!

There is a place to unravel and a plan for reducing the tempo. Step one is to travel across the border to the tiny Mexican village of Tecate, about fifty miles southeast of San Diego in Baja California. In this 2" x 4" town are two "industries," beer-brewing and Rancho La Puerta. As businesses go, they are dissimilar, but together they really do boost Mexico's economy.

The Ranch, with a staff of one hundred to care for one hundred and fifty guests, is a health spa. What, no cheering? Does the thought of health and pampering turn you off? Or does your schedule make it impossible? Then think of it as a vacation; prices are about the same or less than what you'd pay for a hotel room. Listen to more. It's not for women only and children are also welcome; it's an uncrowded family affair, and you won't be conscious of people around you. The *ranchitas* (cabins) are spread out and tucked away in vineyard valleys. Singles find pleasure with the varied clientele at La Puerta and show biz names take their minds and bodies there to turn off the pace as nowhere else can.

We like the family idea. It's good to play together, kiting or any other sport: to become conversationalists as opposed to TV addicts: to stretch muscles in exercise, and then at dusk flex wits in philosophical duels; or simply to chatter. And the most appealing idea is getting to know oneself and one's mate once again. That's really good.

The food is good, too. Even though you may fear that health spa diet desparation, it doesn't exist at Rancho La Puerta, the distaff side of the team that started La Puerta over thirty years ago is a petite blond super-charged woman well ahead of her time in ideas (many of her successes have been duplicated elsewhere,) who goes by the name of Deborah Szekely (pronounced See-ky.) Vegetarianism and organically grown products are not new at La Puerta where the idea is over a quarter of a century old! Many people do go to the Ranch for weight loss (five pounds a week is average and for safety's sake,) but for those who want to gain or stay the same there's appetite-satiating food, and everybody from time to time enjoys yum-yumming some freshly baked-in-a-stone-outdoor oven bread dripping with honey.

A well-planned diet, with exercise, is a giant step to physical fitness; it's great for the body and the complexion. Take a Rancho La Puerta family health resort vacation, or serve this sample vegetarian luncheon menu at home. For the majority, it will be a tummy-easer, much as kite flying and hammock swinging are tension easers. You'll see.

RANCHO LA PUERTA LUNCHEON

Rollatini di Zucchini
Coeurs D'Artichauts
Sauce de Tomate au Michel
Fraises D'Australie

A delicious vegetarian entrée, the sauce is very flavorful and the filling, like the entire dish, is low calorie, good for you and tasty. It is also a colorful dish to serve for luncheon with steamed white or brown rice and perhaps a few marinated artichoke hearts. Finish the meal off with Australian Strawberries, the dieter's version of Strawberries Romanoff...your friends will never know the difference between the two recipes, so keep it under your Aussie hat.

ROLLATINI DI ZUCCHINI
Stuffed Zucchini Rolls

Sauce de Tomate au Michel, see Index
4 small (about 5 to 6 inches) zucchini squash
3/4 cup ricotta cheese
1 slice tomato, peeled and finely chopped
2 tablespoons finely chopped onion
2 tablespoons finely chopped parsley
1 1/2 teaspoons finely chopped chives
Salt substitute (or salt) and pepper to taste
Dash of nutmeg
Grated Parmesan cheese

Prepare Sauce de Tomate first. It can be simmering while next part of recipe is being made. Trim off and discard ends of zucchini. Split each one in half; using a melon ball cutter or grapefruit spoon, scoop out center pulp and reserve. Prepare stuffing by combining cheese, tomato, onion, parsley, chives and seasoning. Chop pulp finely and mix with other filling ingredients. When sauce is done, remove two tablespoonfuls of sauce to add to filling for a prettier coloring. Blend in well. Prepare a shallow baking dish, of a suitable size to hold eight zucchini halves, by greasing it lightly. (This can be a bake and serve dish, if desired.) Stuff each zucchini with filling in a slightly rounded or puffed looking way. Before placing zucchini in baking dish, put some sauce on bottom of dish, then set in zucchini. Top each zucchini half with sauce

111

and pour any remaining around the sides of the vegetables. Cover loosely with foil and place in preheated 350° oven for 30 to 45 minutes checking for tenderness at 20 minutes to judge total cooking time. Remove foil, sprinkle tops of zucchini halves with grated Parmesan cheese and serve. Makes 4 generous servings.

COEURS D'ARTICHAUTS
Hearts of Artichokes

1 can (8 1/2 ounces) artichoke hearts, about 10 to 12 hearts,
*   or 1 package frozen artichoke hearts, cooked*
1 tablespoon lemon juice
1 tablespoon white wine vinegar
1 1/2 tablespoons cold-pressed corn oil
2 teaspoons chopped chives
2 teaspoons chopped parsley
1 shallot, minced or crushed

If using canned artichokes, drain juices and reserve vegetables in small bowl. If frozen artichoke hearts are used prepare according to package instructions. Combine remaining ingredients in a cup or small bowl and pour over hearts. Place in refrigerator jar to chill for 4 or more hours. Turn container upside down part of the time to let marinade reach all of the hearts to season. Serve cold. Makes 4 servings.

FRAISES D'AUSTRALIE
Australian Strawberries

2 cups strawberries, washed, stemmed and quartered
1/4 cup Grand Marnier
2 teaspoons Sweet'n Low sugar substitute
1 envelope (1 1/4 ounces) Low Calorie Whipped Topping

Prepare berries. In small saucepan over low heat, bring Grand Marnier to boil. Continue boiling until all alcohol has evaporated. Pour liqueur into cup containing sugar substitute to dissolve it and cool liqueur. Prepare Whipped Topping according to package directions using skim milk or well-chilled water. Pour Grand Marnier over strawberries to mix well. Fold berries into Whipped Topping. Serve at once, or cover bowl and set overnight in refrigerator to let the strawberries and liqueur flavors wed. Makes 4 to 6 servings.

SAUCES

ACAPULCO SAUCE (GRANT GRILL)

1 small yellow chili pepper
3 medium tomatoes
4 sprigs fresh cilantro, optional*
1/2 cup tomato juice
1/4 teaspoon white pepper
1 teaspoon salt
1/4 teaspoon monosodium
1 teaspoon Worcestershire sauce

Hold chili pepper over a flame and broil it, or place it on surface of medium hot electric range unit until it has become spotted from the heat. Remove and wrap in a towel or heavy paper bag to let steam for 15 minutes. Then peel skin, remove core and seeds. Chop finely and place in bowl. Quickly scald tomatoes in boiling water until skins can be easily removed. Peel completely and chop finely, adding to bowl with chili. Chop cilantro (or parsley), add it with juice and seasonings to bowl contents. Let stand until serving time.

*Cilantro, also known as coriander, is a Mexican or Chinese type of parsley. Some people find it too pungent and prefer the American double-curled variety.

Note: This sauce is another fine Mexican dip to serve as an appetizer with tostados (corn chips). It also is a refreshing and different condiment for beef, pork and chicken.

113

BAR-B-Q SAUCE OR FRENCH DRESSING (SARRETT HOUSE)

1 cup water
1/2 cup sugar
1 clove garlic, split
1/2 cup vinegar
1 cup chili sauce
1/4 cup (2 ounces) horseradish
1 1/2 teaspoons salt
1 tablespoon prepared Dijon mustard
1 teaspoon celery salt
1 cup oil for buffalo or dry non-fatty type meats for
*   sauce or 1/2 cup oil for dressing*

Combine water, sugar and garlic; boil in saucepan over medium heat for 5 minutes. Add remaining ingredients; mix well. Let stand unchilled for basting meats. Refrigerate. Makes 3 3/4 cups dressing, or 4 1/4 cups sauce.

BECHAMEL SAUCE (THE MAD GREEK'S)

3 tablespoons butter
3 tablespoons flour
3 cups hot milk
3 egg yolks, beaten
Dash of nutmeg
Salt to taste

Melt butter in saucepan, blend in flour. Add milk all at once, beat vigorously with wire whisk. Simmer over low heat; stir frequently. Cook about 10 minutes. Pour a little white sauce into egg yolks; return mixture to sauce. Over medium-low heat, cook and stir briskly until thickened; season. Makes about 3 1/2 cups sauce.

Note: This sauce may be used as a basic sauce or binding sauce for creamed dishes. It is good with vegetables and hot poultry, eggs and veal.

CABRILLO SAUCE (LUBACH'S)

1/2 cup butter
1 teaspoon dry mustard
1 bottle (14 ounces) ketchup
Juice of 1 lemon
5 dashes Worcestershire sauce
2 dashes Tabasco sauce

Melt butter in saucepan; do not brown it. Blend in mustard and cook a few minutes over low heat. Add remaining ingredients and bring to a boil. Reduce heat and simmer 20 minutes to blend flavors. Makes about 2 1/2 cups sauce.

Note: This sauce is good as a seasoning for all meats and outdoor cooking.

CUYAMACA SAUCE

2 yolks hard-cooked eggs
1 whole uncooked egg
2 teaspoons dry mustard
2 tablespoons heavy cream
1 cup olive oil
1 tablespoon cider vinegar
1 tablespoon lemon juice
1/2 teaspoon salt
1/4 teaspoon pepper
1/4 teaspoon monosodium glutamate

Use a blender with various speeds or an electric mixer (you'll need one hand free). In blender or mixing bowl place yolks, uncooked egg, mustard, and cream, and blend quickly. Pour oil drop by drop into mixture while blender is whizzing or beaters are going (at a speed that will whip but not cause splashing) until mixture builds up like mayonnaise. Stir in vinegar, lemon juice and seasonings. Place, covered, in refrigerator, unless using immediately. For sauce over hot fish it should be lukewarm;

as an appetizer dip for vegetables or seafood it should be chilled. Makes about 1 2/3 cups Sauce.

Note: A more spirited dip may be made by the addition of capers, anchovies and garlic (optional). To do so, blend in (after the addition of the cream) 6 tablespoons (1 bottle) drained capers, 1 can (2-ounce size) anchovy filets, and 1 clove garlic, coarsely chopped. This sauce or dip is known as Tapenade (Tapena is *Provençal* for capers). To serve, place attractive cuts of vegetables and/or seafood in a serving platter filled with a bed of crushed ice; offer chilled Tapenade Sauce in a bowl.

Crudités are the French way with crisp raw vegetables. The ones that are best with this sauce are fennel, Belgian endive, celery, turnips, radishes, carrots, cherry tomatoes, celery root, zucchini and the Mexican vegetable, jicama. It is also delightful as a dip for cooked, chilled lobster, shrimp or crabmeat.

FIORENTINA SAUCE (BOCACCIO'S)
2 cloves garlic, crushed
1/4 pound fresh mushrooms, finely sliced
1/4 pound butter
1/4 cup dry red wine
1 tablespoon finely chopped fresh parsley

In a medium skillet sauté garlic and mushrooms in butter over medium temperature. After about 10 minutes, when mushrooms are softened, add wine.Let bubble up, then simmer for 10 more minutes. Stir in parsley. Set aside until serving time. Makes about 1 cup Sauce, enough for 4 servings.

GUACAMOLE SUPREME (TOM HAM'S LIGHTHOUSE)

1 1/2 medium size ripe avocados, mashed
1/2 medium onion, minced
1/2 bunch cilantro, finely chopped (optional)
4 medium tomatoes

116

Juice of 1/2 lemon, strained
1/2 teaspoon salt
1/4 teaspoon white pepper
1/4 teaspoon monosodium glutamate
Dash of Tabasco sauce

In a bowl combine avocado, onion and cilantro. Chop one tomato very finely and add to bowl contents with seasonings. Stir to blend thoroughly. Place remaining tomatoes briefly in boiling water to loosen skins; peel. Cut each tomato in half, spread or heap Guacamole dip on top (a pastry bag may be used to create a design, if desired). Place in refrigerator to chill until ready to use as a garnish. Makes 4 to 6 servings.

Note: The Guacamole may be served in a bowl as a dip with tostados (corn chips). Use only one tomato in ingredients instead of four as suggested above, since halved tomatoes are for garnish not dip.

HOLLANDAISE SAUCE (EARL'S)

2 tablespoons butter
3 egg yolks
2 tablespoons water
Juice of 1/2 lemon, strained
3 to 4 drops Tabasco sauce

Melt butter in skillet and set aside. Use heavy saucepan or double boiler for cooking egg yolks (keep water scant in bottom pan). Remove white cords from yolks, beat vigorously with water in pan; cook over low heat. Do not let eggs boil; remove pan from heat as necessary. Continue to whip while adding butter slowly. Beat again. When thickened pour in juice gradually. Heat and remove; add Tabasco and taste for seasoning. Cover top of pan with plastic wrap to prevent coating from forming and set aside. Makes about 1 cup sauce.

Note: This sauce is good with many vegetables such as asparagus, broccoli and artichokes.

Courtesy of Bob Perine

MADEIRA WINE SAUCE (PUCCI'S)

2 1/2 cups prepared Brown Sauce (or canned brown gravy)
1/4 cup Madeira wine
2 tablespoons (about 1 small can) minced truffles
Salt and pepper to taste

Heat Brown Sauce in saucepan; simmer uncovered until reduced to about 1 3/4 cups. Remove from heat; add wine, truffles and seasoning. Reheat before serving. Makes about 2 cups sauce.

Note: This sauce is also good with roasts, other meats and potatoes.

MORNAY SAUCE (ATLANTIS)

2 tablespoons butter, melted
2 tablespoons flour
1 1/2 cups hot milk
1/2 cup grated Parmesan cheese

In a saucepan over medium heat, make a roux by blending flour into butter. Slowly add hot milk. Stir until thickened; add cheese and stir through to be certain cheese is melted. Let stand until ready to serve. Makes about 2 cups sauce.

PROVENCALE SAUCE (ATLANTIS)

1 tablespoon oil
1 clove garlic, minced or crushed
1 shallot, minced or crushed
1 cup dry white wine
3 medium tomatoes, peeled, seeded and chopped
1 teaspoon dry thyme leaves
1/2 teaspoon dry basil leaves
1/2 teaspoon salt
1/2 teaspoon monosodium glutamate
1/4 teaspoon pepper
Pinch of sugar

Sauté the garlic and shallot in saucepan with oil. When lightly browned add wine and tomatoes. Add seasonings and sugar; stir to mix well. Simmer gently over medium to low heat for half an hour. Mixture should be pulpy, not runny in consistency. Makes about 1 to 1 1/2 cups sauce.

RED SWEET-SOUR SAUCE (CHINA LAND)

1/4 cup water
2 tablespoons cherry juice, pineapple juice or water
1 1/2 tablespoons ketchup
1/2 cup sugar
1/4 teaspoon salt
1/2 cup vinegar
2 1/4 teaspoons cornstarch
1/4 teaspoon red food coloring

Bring water, juice and ketchup to boil. Add sugar and salt, stirring, and cook a minute or two until dissolved. Add 1/3 cup vinegar and cook 1 minute longer. Blend remaining vinegar to a paste with cornstarch. Stir cornstarch mixture into saucepan, add food coloring. Stir and cook (do not boil) until thickened and clear. Makes about 1 1/2 cups sauce.

Note: This sauce is good with many Chinese dishes such as spare-ribs, chicken and shrimp.

SALSA FRESCA (TOM HAM'S LIGHTHOUSE)

2 medium bell peppers
2 medium dry onions
3 medium carrots, parboiled (but firm)
8 green onions
1 medium tomato
1/2 bunch cilantro, optional
1/2 teaspoon salt
1/2 teaspoon cracked black pepper

1 *teaspoon ground cumin*
1 *teaspoon oregano*
1/2 *teaspoon monosodium glutamate*

Slice vegetables in short strips, julienne style; chop cilantro and add to vegetables, add seasonings and let stand until serving time.

Note: This sauce is another fine Mexican dip to serve as an appetizer with tostados (corn chips). It also is a refreshing and different condiment for beef, pork and chicken.

SAUCE DE TOMATE AU MICHEL
Tomato Sauce, Michel

1/4 *onion, finely chopped*
1 *shallot, minced*
1 *garlic clove, minced*
3 *teaspoons cold-pressed corn oil*
1 *can (1 pound) tomatoe purée*
2 *teaspoons oregano*
2 *bay leaves*
2 *teaspoons parsley, finely chopped*
Salt substitute (or salt)
White pepper, to taste

In a medium saucepan over medium heat sauté onion, shallot and garlic in oil. When vegetables are limp add remaining ingredients, including bay leaves and oregano. Do not add other seasonings. Simmer 30 minutes; stir occasionally to prevent sticking. Just before serving add parsley and seasoning. Makes about 2 cups sauce.

SOUR CREAM SAUCE (MI BURRO)

1 1/2 *whole (canned) green Ortega chiles*
1/2 *fresh tomato, cut up*
1/4 *small onion, cut up*

1 *clove garlic*
1 *pint dairy sour cream*
Salt to taste

Remove seeds from chiles, cut up and put in blender with tomato, onion and garlic. Whizz until ingredients form a paste. Blend paste into sour cream with salt. (Do not whip sour cream in blender). Spoon sauce over enchiladas. Makes about 2 1/4 cups sauce.

Note: This sour cream mix makes a delicious dip. Make it ahead of time; store in refrigerator until needed. Serve chilled with tostados (corn chips).

TARRAGON SAUCE MOUSSELINE (FONTAINEBLEAU)

1 1/2 *tablespoons white wine*
1 *shallot, minced*
1 *teaspoon fresh chopped tarragon leaves or 1/2 teaspoon*
    dried tarragon
3 *egg yolks, slightly beaten*
1/3 *cup clarified butter or melted sweet butter*
Salt and pepper to taste
1/2 *cup chilled whipping cream*

In a saucepan over low heat simmer the wine, shallot and tarragon very slowly. With a wire whisk beat in egg yolks, whipping constantly. Still beating, add butter very slowly, as for Hollandaise. Cool sauce; adjust for seasoning (seasoning will be diluted by addition of cream later). Just before time to pour over veal, whip cream and fold into sauce. Pour over veal and other ingredients on warm platter. Glaze under broiler to a mellow yellow. Makes about 1 3/4 cups sauce.

Note: This sauce is also good with fish, soufflés and vegetables.

VINAIGRETTE SAUCE (LA COSTA)

1 large sweet green pepper, finely chopped
2 green onions, finely chopped
1 jar (2 ounces) diced pimientos
1 cup unsweetened apple juice
1/2 cup white vinegar
1/4 cup lemon juice
About 3 drops diet liquid sweetener or one packet
*   powdered (equivalent to 2 teaspoons sugar)*
*   sweetner, to taste*
Dash of white pepper

Combine ingredients. Let stand one half hour or longer to blend flavors. Pour sauce over sliced cucumbers, sliced beets, or use as a salad dressing. Makes 2 cups sauce; one-half this amount is sufficient for four to six persons in combination with salad vegetables. This is a good sauce to keep refrigerated for other occasions; for example, an interesting salad can be prepared with this sauce and cooked shrimp.

WINES FROM ALTO AND BAJA CALIFORNIA

To discuss California wines one should start at the bottom and work up, from away down in Mexico that is. For with the Spaniards' arrival in the New World came the grape and the art of winemaking. That was in the seventeenth century, and soon after the Jesuits moved on across the Gulf of Mexico into the Baja peninsula. There, near the community of Loreto, they built the first mission in lower California; and around it they established self-sustaining agriculture and planted the first seedlings of the sacramental grape. In time this *Monica* grape of Spain, later quite aptly dubbed by vintners the Mission grape, since it was the only variety the missions did cultivate, flourished sufficiently to supply wine to the fifteen then-existing Jesuit missions.

At first it may seem inappropriate to think of wine in connection with religion and government, but that's the way it is when we delve into the histories of California's vineyards. For example, in 1768 the Jesuits lost favor with the Pope and were banished from Mexico. The Order packed off to Russia to remain until the year 1814. Meanwhile two other religious orders, the Franciscans and the Dominicans, took over where the Jesuits left off, splitting the territory according to their own compromise. The Dominicans were to adopt the Jesuit missions extending from Loreto into the North, and the Franciscans planned to develop Alto California.

125

Father Junipero Serra, the historical figure so well-known for his *El Camino Real,* established a chain of twenty-one missions beginning with San Diego in 1769 and ending in Sonoma in 1823. Each mission was built a traveling day apart, and where agriculture was feasible, and if weather was beneficial, the blue-black *Monica* grapes were also planted. During the same time, the Dominicans expanded the former Jesuit territory in Baja California and by 1794 they had built their northernmost mission in Santo Tomas Valley, not far from the unbelievable lush-green Guadalupe Valley, an inland area over a barrier knoll from the sea. La Mison de Santo Tomas has long suffered from disrepair and by now is little more than a crumbled heap of time-eroded bricks, but the grapes did survive.

Finally, by 1930, General Abelardo Rodriguez, a businessman, soldier, Governor of Sonora, Mexico, and two-year term President of Mexico, had acquired all of the lands and the old winery. Much work was done restoring the vineyards and Rodriguez built the *bodegas* (wine cellars) in Ensenada, forty miles north of Santo Tomas, because of the port facilities and available electricity. Santo Tomas Valley still has no electricity!

Attempts were continually made to introduce the familiar varietal grapes of Alto California, but not until the arrival of Dmitri Tchelistcheff (to pronounce correctly, omit the "t's" and it's a snap) was this accomplished. Mr. Tchelistcheff became Wine Master of Santo Tomas in 1963. He is a graduate of the University of California at Davis and the son of André Tchelistcheff, one of the most respected oenologists in the Napa Valley. Because of his modesty you would probably never hear about Dmitri's greatly admired professional skill from his own lips. However, he is considered important enough in his ability to discern minute taste differences that he was a consultant in selecting the kinds of champagne that President Nixon took with him to China this year.

But to return to the *bodegas.* Dmitri has so improved the vineyards and upgraded the winery that today Santo

Tomas produces twenty varieties of wine, plus the bub-
bly and the brandy. To roam through the wine cellars
in Ensenada is to walk through a giant maze. The cellars
are so vast, it's easy to see how one and one-half million
gallons of wine can be aged in 20,000 gallon casks for the
extensive periods necessary. And Dmitri is planning to
expand. Another building is being constructed to house
several new casks he has just bought from a California
winery that is converting to stainless steel. These wooden
casks will be shipped down in marked jig-saw pieces and
reassembled at the bodegas, for Dmitri takes parental
pride in the slow-aging process necessary in these mam-
moth old oaken casks. His equipment also includes complete facilities for making bottle-fermented champagne,
including riddling racks.

Speaking of pride, Dmitri has a sparkling rosé wine
that is outstanding in flavor and is uniquely developed
by natural fermentation. The vinification process begins
with a *cuvée* of 100% Grenache grapes. The fermentation
is carefully controlled at 45°F. until the slight residual
sugar content is reached. Then the temperature is low-
ered to just above freezing, which retains the natural
carbon dioxide gas in the wine and traps the bubbles.
The tanks are then sealed until bottling time, and even
then it is unnecessary to add carbonation for appearance
or taste. This rosé is a rose is a rose.

Soft-spoken and uncomplaining, Dmitri has had an up-
hill road all the way. His every need in the winery has of
necessity to be imported, except for the grapes. Bottles
travel from Spain, corks from Portugal and labels from
Mexico City. Then, when the vintage is *listo* (ready), the
bottles are filled, corked and labeled, and packed in cases
to be trucked up to Tijuana and other border towns, or up
to Mexicali to follow the direct route south three days
and nights to the main distribution point, Mexico City.
It's a good thing that Santo Tomas wines travel well,
for this winery has a growing number of aficionados.
Currently there are seven wines imported into California
through distributors. The selected wines available in the

United States may be ordered through the House of Sobel in San Francisco, Young's Market in Los Angeles or Young's Market (local offices), 1709 Main Street, San Diego, California 92113. The wines may be purchased directly through several San Diego liquor stores and are served in border-town Mexico restaurants and many local Mexican cuisine restaurants. Santo Tomás maintains two vineyards, one at Rancho de Los Dolores in Santo Tomás Valley, the other in Guadalupe Valley. The winery, Bodegas de Santo Tomás, is at 666 Avenida Miramar, Ensenada, Baja California, Mexico.

In the former Franciscan territory of San Diego County, the crush is on...not the fall *crush* that produces juice from the grapes, but instead a gradual reduction in number of vineyards. In the early 1900's there were thirty five wineries; now there are two. This is attributed to land subdivision developments, increased irrigation costs, and taxes. It's a real pity to see them go, for if and when the last two wineries vanish, so does a bit of California history.

Once, according to Mission records, the Bernardo winery land was part of the grazing rancho of the San Diego Mission de Alcala. In 1769 that area was known as El Parajo o Canada de San Bernardo. After the 1830 revolution the Mission land was taken, but later, during the terms of two different Mexican governors, parcels were deeded to a certain J. F. Snook, an English sea captain. At his death he left extensive holdings but no heirs. And the property was sold in 1882.

Five Italian partners bought about 310 acres of the property and operated it as a winery until 1932. In 1933 when the partnership split up, Vincent Rizzo, a Sicilian descended from generations of vintners, bought the land and expanded its production. Now Ross Rizzo, his son, runs the business as Rizzo and Son Bernardo Winery. With only 150 acres remaining of the original land, he and a single helper tend the entire operation from the pruning and picking of the grapes to the production of the wines.

Bernardo Winery produces fifteen varieties of wine, including the Monica grape dark red claret. All of the Rizzo processing is done naturally and aged in huge redwood casks for about two to three years before selling. Of particular interest to persons concerned with organically grown foods, the Rizzo vineyard is not treated with chemicals, herbicides or fertilizers. The plants are lush and green when it is not picking or pruning season, and some of the vines are over eighty-five years old. In alternating rows there are olive trees, just as one might imagine the Franciscans had planted around their missions when they settled in California. For their sacramental needs included planting grape vines for wine and olive trees for oil. The grape harvest is done in the fall months of the year, and from December through February it's olive time. Then the clear oil is extracted by the cold-press method.

Bernardo Winery may be visited, and personalized tours are conducted upon request. They have a tasting room which is open daily and all of their products are for sale on the premises. You will find the winery six miles south of Escondido. It is a short distance from U.S. Highway 395; east at Pomerado Road off-ramp (by Lake Hodges Bridge), two miles to the sign indicating the winery, and a turn left on a dirt road for one-half mile.

Another grazing rancho of the late 1700's, the Rancho Rincon del Diablo is the site of a centrally located winery that has survived to this date. The majority of land became Escondido, and at the beginning of the twentieth century the economy of Escondido was based on the grape industry. During Prohibition the many vintners in the area took to supplying grapes for table use and shipped their products by rail (which took longer and incurred greater loss), but one George Ferrar trucked his to Los Angeles in a quick twelve hours! (Times and speeds have surely changed.)

As a result George Ferrar earned the title of Mr. Grapes. In 1932 he established his own Ferrara Winery almost in the midst of Escondido, and although he has retired to some degree, he continues his interest in the winery and its development. Gaspar Ferrar, his son, took over the responsibility of management and became the wine master in 1951, and in the past twenty years his other two sons, Anthony and George, also became assistants in this family owned winery.

Although their vineyard has shrunk, the Ferrars keep their production high. They buy grapes from nearby growers and others in Ramona, Fallbrook and the De Luz valley, sometimes even as far away as Bloomington in Riverside County. But meanwhile quality has remained their most important asset, and it is achieved primarily by consistent aging in redwood and oak barrels. They have upped their number of wines produced to twenty two, including a specialty, developed by George Ferrar Sr., called Vino di Caspano. This is a heavy-bodied red table wine made from the Carignane grape. From it they also make a superb marinade for meats, and if you visit the winery, you must be sure to buy a bottle to take home and try in cooking.

Ferrara Winery is located in Escondido at 1120 5th Street, and you may tour or visit their tasting room which is open daily from 8:30 A.M. to 7:30 P.M. Mrs. Gaspar Ferrar or some member of the family is usually present to extend a warm welcome, so do visit when you're in the area. From U. S. Highway 395 turn west at 17th Avenue and travel to Redwood Street; turn toward 15th Avenue, and at 15th continue west to the winery.

Although Father Serra did not build any mission in Escondido, the area did become a leading vineyard ranchland in the ensuing two hundred years. And recently the State of California has recognized both Bernardo and Ferrara Wineries and marked them as historical points of interest.. Moreover, one of the best ways to learn about wines is to visit an operating winery, especially during the crush season; for although this is their busiest time of year, it is the most educational time for observing the simple and complex features of oenology procedures.

130

The ACAPULCO

Just how many restaurants can afford a full-time artist on the premises? You laugh. But it's true; the Acapulco has a man named Joe Maille who spends each day in his "shop" there, or researching at the Oceanside Public Library. Between the two places he manages to produce remarkable duplications of early Aztec and Mayan civilization artifacts. To achieve his perfectionistic realism he works at imperfection, and he creates his own work materials, which have tremendous durability. Most of his many simultaneous projects take a good six months to finish, but time is no criterion for Mr. Maille, who came to Oceanside to escape the smog and rat race in Los Angeles.

About five years ago Jerry Stapp, the owner, with an art-appreciation-eye met Joe Maille, the chemist, historian and artist in need of a "shop" spot. They quickly found rapport and now Jerry's restaurant is the beneficiary. Joe has created the beautifully grained, friendly round tables and Jerry has surrounded them with comfortable black leather chairs to relax in. It's no "Hasty Pudding" type Mexican restaurant, it's more what you'd see in Mexico City. Mr. Stapp has chosen comfort and quality over quantity in every direction...most unusual in today's restaurant business. But, then, he too is no ordinary man. He is from an old German family who arrived in California by the overland route, and the family can at present boast five living generations here. While San Diego was celebrating its 200th anniversary, it made him a Don, because of these unusual circumstances. During World War II Jerry Stapp was in Counter-Intelligence under General Eisenhower, and later, as the civilian part-owner of Patio La Mace in Denver, Colorado (in 1952), his restaurant was selected for the press party celebrating newly elected President Eisenhower and his running mate, Vice-President Nixon. Small world. His family cheese cake recipe (given here) was served then, and ever since he has had innumerable requests for it.

The Acapulco restaurant is evidence of the bond of friendship that exists between Jerry Stapp and Joe Maille. Joe has made his presence known outside and inside, in large carvings and in smaller silk-screen menus. As for Jerry Stapp, his restaurant management and affability speak for the regulars who come to forget problems or the time of day, to change their menu or simply to relax in ideal surroundings. You can escape, too, when you visit this Acapulco.

If you ever have a yen for real home made cheese pie or cake, not the kind you usually find in restaurants, this is it. At the Acapulco, where the Mexican cuisine is very fine, they serve a choice of only two desserts, this cheese pie and ice cream. The recipe is a Stapp family heritage, and here are some of the secrets about it.

CHEESE PIE (OR CAKE)

1/4 cup confectioners' sugar
1 teaspoon cinnamon
3/4 cup butter
1 1/4 cups coarsely crushed graham crackers

Stir sugar and cinnamon into mixing bowl containing crackers. Melt butter in small saucepan over low heat; add butter to cracker mixture. Confectioners' sugar is preferred as it is never gritty as regular sugar sometimes is. Place mixture in 9-inch pie pan and pat evenly around it; be sure crust is not thick in some areas and thin in others. Prepare filling.

Filling:

3 eggs, slightly beaten

1/2 cup sugar
Pinch of salt
14 ounces (1 8-ounce package and 2 3-ounce packages)
    soft cream cheese
1 tablespoon reconstituted lemon juice
1 teaspoon vanilla

Beat eggs with sugar and salt; add pieces of cream cheese and beat well until smooth. Add seasonings; blend well. Reconstituted lemon juice is preferred because of its consistency. Fresh lemon juice may be either tart or almost sweet, and Mr. Stapp feels that using this particular lemon juice introduces the lemon flavor without it being overpowering. Pour filling into prepared crust. Bake in preheated 350° oven for one-half hour, until firm. Remove it and cool it. Preheat oven to 450°. Prepare topping.

Topping:

1 cup dairy sour cream
1/4 cup sugar
1 teaspoon vanilla
1 tablespoon confectioners' sugar

Mix together above ingredients, except for confectioners' sugar; do not beat. When pie is lukewarm, spread mixture across top of filling. Flash bake in preheated oven about 5 minutes to glaze surface to a golden tone. Cool it. Sprinkle with confectioners' sugar, for eye appeal not for more sugar. Cover with plastic wrap and refrigerate until serving time. It should set for about 4 to 6 hours. Makes 12 medium size servings.

In San Diego the Cuyamaca Club serves a good variation of Strawberries Romanoff. It's their traveling maître d'hôtel's German version.

STRAWBERRIES ROMANOFF (CUYAMACA)*

Sauce Romanoff, see Index
4 cups (2 baskets) fresh strawberries
1/3 cup (or more) sugar
2 tablespoons Kirsch
1/2 cup Grand Marnier
1/4 cup orange curaçao

Prepare Sauce Romanoff. Clean berries, remove stems and add sugar according to tartness. Let stand about an hour to let berries absorb sugar. Thirty minutes before serving add mixture of Kirsch, Grand Marnier and orange curaçao; chill in covered container. To serve spoon a little Sauce Romanoff into bottom of brandy snifters, dessert or parfait glasses; add drained strawberries, reserving six or eight pretty berries for garnishing. Spoon remaining sauce over berries. Top each serving with a single berry. Makes 6 to 8 servings.

*This recipe first appeared in SERVE IT COLD! published by Doubleday & Company, Inc., 1969. Co-authored by June Crosby and Ruth Conrad Bateman.

This is a Sarrett House dessert that everyone enjoys. It is excellent as they serve it with fresh or canned fruit. I have found it equally appealing on vanilla-flavored custards such as the convenient ready or almost ready puddings; and it's a delight over the good old standbys, rice, blanc mange and tapioca. Use it sparingly, but enjoy the zingy flavor thoroughly.

FRUIT WITH LEMON CURD SAUCE

Fresh or canned fruit
1 recipe Lemon Curd Sauce, see Index

Serve fruit in dessert or parfait glasses. Pour a little sauce on top, or pass in sauce bowl at the table. Makes 4 to 6 servings.

Persimmon pudding is a favorite of ours, and you'll become a fan once you try it at Sarrett House or in your own home. It's my guess you'll wish persimmons were available all year around.

PERSIMMON PUDDING, SARRETT HOUSE

1 cup sifted flour
1 cup sugar
2 teaspoon baking soda
1/2 teaspoon cinnamon
1/2 cup milk
1 egg, beaten
1 cup persimmon pulp
2 tablespoons butter, melted
Sugar
Whipped cream or hard sauce for topping

Sift together dry ingredients. Whisk egg into milk; blend this mixture into persimmon pulp and butter which have been combined. Grease inside of steamed pudding mold (or use small cans with well fitting lids), sprinkle inside of mold with sugar and fill mold (or cans) about 2/3 full. Cover and place mold on trivet or rack in a heavy saucepan with at least one inch of water in it. Cover saucepan and steam on range top for 2 hours. When done persimmon pudding should test dry with toothpick.

An alternate method is to prepare pudding as above and place in baking dish in preheated 325° oven. Bake about one hour, until done. Serve with whipped cream or hard sauce for topping. Makes 4 servings.

上海飯店 SHANGHAI

What's the "in" thing this year in clothes, conversation and cuisine? China, of course. And what's painted red all over, trimmed in bamboo, and decorated with black characters that spell out good food from China's various provinces? That's La Jolla's new Shanghai. It's aptly named, for Shanghai (the city) is noted for offering a melting pot of Chinese cookery styles in its restaurants.

Proprietor Cheng Sheng Tien, from Chungking, has brought distinction to his restaurant by elevating it from the typical American chop suey place to a real Chinese dining room that could be likened to a restaurant in Taiwan, Hong Kong, or Shanghai. Tien takes one's jaded appetite, presents a selection of predominately Mandarin and Cantonese cuisines, and lets you be rewarded by savoring contrasts in aroma, color and texture.

In America we prepare a food, such as beans, in many different ways from North to South and East to West, and these methods could be spoken of as our various schools of cooking. The same is true in China, where five great schools of cooking are known to exist. Tien has brought two of these, the Peking-Shantung (Mandarin) and Southeastern (Cantonese) to San Diego's attention. Their basic differences are in types of seasonings, cooking methods and specialty dishes. Together the Mandarin and Cantonese styles make palatable music to gourmets of Chinese foods.

We Americans relate to the Cantonese style, as Chinese from that area were first to emigrate to our shores; but a Shanghai dinner such as Tien suggests gives a much better example of the variety of regional Chinese cuisine. To feast à la Tien, after cocktails try Sizzling Rice Soup . . . a blend of chicken broth, shrimp, mushrooms and abalone, with crips chunks of crusty rice dropped straight into the bowl from a sizzling pan by

138

your waiter. Then order some wine with appetizers of
Moo-Shi Pork . . . shredded pork and water chestnuts
wrapped in a large thin pancake, or Barbecued Chicken
Salad . . . chicken combined with rice, noodles, lettuce,
red ginger and eight different spices.

For main courses to share, order Kung Poa Chicken . . .
diced chicken, peanuts, red pepper and brown sauce;
Crackling Shrimp . . . shelled shrimp, snow peas and
bamboo shoots served over crackling hot rice; and Peking
Duck . . . a whole duck, honey dipped and barbecued to
a crisp golden brown. And if that doesn't send you cry-
ing "Uncle!," finish the feast with a devastating dessert
requested all over the Orient, Chinese Candied Apples.

These may be similar to Hallowe'en treats, but similar
is all; for these are delectable slices of apple rolled in
batter, deep-fried, cooked and coated in a honey syrup,
then quickly dipped by your waiter into ice water just
before serving. They become golden, crunchy and mellow tidbits, and you won't forget them.

CHINESE CANDIED APPLES

2 egg whites, unbeaten
2 tablespoons flour
2 tablespoons cornstarch
2 crisp large apples, peeled and cored
Oil for deep-frying
2 tablespoons oil (peanut preferred)
1 cup sugar
1/2 cup water
2 tablespoons corn syrup

Make a batter of egg whites, flour and cornstarch; add
water, if needed, to thin batter for better consistency.
Slice apples lengthwise in 1/2-inch pieces. Dip in batter
to coat. Heat oil for deep-frying to 400°; place apples in
fryer with basket to hold them. Fry to pale golden. Drain
on paper toweling. In a saucepan combine oil, sugar,

water and syrup. Boil syrup over high heat to 240° on candy thermometer. Add fruit when temperature is reached and cook only until syrup begins to brown and starts to carmelize (about 3 to 4 minutes). Stir fruit gently; do not let syrup burn. Rub serving platter generously with oil (to keep fruit from sticking). Turn out fruit and syrup onto platter; fan to cool slightly. Serve with large bowl of ice cubes in water. To eat, each diner picks up an apple slice with a fork, tongs or chopsticks, dips it quickly in ice water to harden the syrup, then eats it. The fruit keeps it's heat internally, so beware. Makes 4 servings.

Star of the Sea Room

at Anthony's Fish Grotto, San Diego

The name *Star of the Sea* goes back to an ancient legend that tells of a fisherman battered by wind and waves, who, while praying for mercy, had a miraculous vision of the Virgin Mary. She directed him to follow a brilliant star, and he found a secure harbor. Ever since then, tempest-tossed sailors have relied on the sacred Stella Maris, or Star of the Sea, as their patron saint.

Today, the name *Star of the Sea* serves another purpose, for it's been the guiding light of Anthony's most deluxe gourmet seafood dining room. Perhaps the ethereal beauty that once inspired sailors to reach safety also directs diners to partake of world-renowned fish and shellfish in this dependable and beautiful restaurant. It's a moot question whether the brilliant stars, or mysterious sea, or olden fables, or man's responsibility to man have most influenced the originality and quality offered by the entire staff of the Star of the Sea Room . . . but whichever it is, originality and quality are omnipresent. From the maître d'hôtel, Marny Di Vries, to the crew that serves at table, to the kitchen with it's fine chefs and aides, this is a smooth, efficient operation done with finesse all the way.

Plan an evening à deux, or with friends you want to impress, and reserve a booth or a table. The armchairs, by the way, are pure luxury with Italian hand-carved wooden frames and gold velvet upholstery. The golden glow of the room is warm and inviting, and the view across San Diego Bay at sunset is positively glorious. The restaurant, part of Anthony's building at the Embarcadero, rests on pilings over the water and there's almost a sensation of being afloat. So if it's elegance, the sea and seafood you are seeking, follow your desires to the Star of the Sea Room and you'll find superlative security awaiting.

Here gourmet seafoods are the forte, including such *rara piscis* as the unique sculpin, the preparation of which is an art; but as an added enticement, maître d'hôtel Marny has contributed a few treats of his own to the menu. Fresh Hawaiian Pineapple à la Marny is one, and it's a perfect non-seasonal dessert to follow a fish or shellfish dinner. Fortunately it adapts to almost any fruit in season, so others may be substituted for the pineapple. It's refreshing and light, and can be made to suit two or twelve.

FRESH HAWAIIAN PINEAPPLE A LA MARNY

1 medium to large pineapple, (or about 3 cups fresh
*   berries or chunks of melon, peaches, pears,*
*   papaya, etc.)*
1/2 pint dairy sour cream
1/2 pint whipped low calorie whip
2 tablespoons brown sugar
1/3 cup Grand Marnier
1/4 cup Orange Curaçao
1 1/2 tablespoons Myers dark rum

Fruit:
Cut pineapple interior into bite-size sections; leave exterior intact for use as serving container. Leave berries whole; cut other fruits into edible pieces. Serve the fruits in a crystal or china bowl.

Dip:
Combine cream with whip; blend brown sugar into Grand Marnier and Orange Curaçao. Add liqueurs to cream mixture; sprinkle with rum.

To Serve:
For two persons it is attractive and fun to serve this dessert as it is done at the Star of the Sea Room. Toothpicks are provided, plus a serving bowl to contain the dip; the pineapple is placed between the diners. Each one takes a toothpick, selects a piece of pineapple, and swizzeling the fruit in the fondue-like dip, eats it, purring with each morsel. But while this method is delightful for two, it's unwieldy for a larger number. I've found with more than two people it is most satisfactory to pass the fruit and sauce for each person to serve himself as much as he wishes in an individual dessert dish. This can also be done from the kitchen; first, place a serving of fruit in the dish, and then spoon a generous portion of the dip. Whichever way, the fresh fruit and the delicately sweet-yet-zingy sauce is bound to be most pleasing. Makes 4 ample servings.

This dessert is just right and light enough for that heavy meal you may have planned. The flavor is almost chocolate-sweet, but interesting and the touch of cinnamon is provocative.

CREME DE CACAO HELADO (VICTOR'S)
Creme de Cacao Ice Cream

1 pint vanilla ice cream

About 1/4 cup creme de cacao, more or less to taste
Cinnamon

Soften vanilla ice cream. Use a blender or mixer and whip in creme de cacao flavoring. Pour into parfait dessert or martini glasses. Garnish each with sprinkling of cinnamon. Serve semi-soft or frozen. Makes 4 to 6 servings; a little of this dessert goes a long way.

LEMON CURD SAUCE* (SARRETT HOUSE)

1/4 cup fresh lemon juice
1/2 teaspoon grated lemon peel
Pinch of salt
2 egg yolks
2 tablespoons butter, melted
1/2 cup sugar

Beat ingredients together. Pour into upper half of double boiler; do not have water touching the bottom of top pan. Cook over medium heat until thickened. Remove sauce from heat. Pour into jar and let stand until cool. Refrigerate until served. This sauce may be kept for several days in refrigerator. Makes 1 cup sauce.

*This sauce is also referred to as Lemon Cheese.

SAUCE ROMANOFF (CUYAMACA)

1 pint vanilla ice cream
1/3 cup cream sherry
1 cup heavy cream, whipped

Soften ice cream by beating quickly in electric mixer. Quickly beat in cream sherry, then fold in whipped cream. Return to freezer a couple of hours before serving. Makes about 3 1/2 cups sauce.

SAN DIEGO CORNUCOPIA

The cuisine of any specific locale tells a lot. It's an illustration of local produce, methods of preparation and styles of cookery. California's culinary heritage has been created from early Spanish and Indian foundations and enhanced by the continuous flow of new people and cultures. In this wacky, western state it's not unusual to cook Mexican dishes, nor to serve home-made chow mein from your own wok. And because of California's seasonal climate, which varies from cold to very warm, and the terrain, which runs from below sea level and barren to very high and fertile, and a coastline that is a vision ad infinitum, this state is unique and varied in food products. Narrowing it down, San Diego is all this and then some.

Agriculture is San Diego's fourth largest indutry, the dollar value of San Diego's products ranks it among the top twenty counties in the nation. Of the 2,700,000 acres in the county, 685,000 are being utilized for this industry. Once, water was a major factor in determining what could be grown; but now, importation of water from other sources has made full use of San Diego's favorable soil and climatic conditions.

Egg production has grown to be the county's most important single agricultural enterprise . . . in fact, San Diego is third in the nation in this field. Close behind on the list are tomatoes, milk and dairy products, and the avocado and citrus industries. The ideal climate and soil for citrus and avocados makes this county one of the world's top areas for these prolific crops.

Of lesser importance, but nonetheless on the scene to make San Diego's produce supply fresher and fancier are celery, strawberries, cucumbers, cabbage and bell peppers. Among the common and exotic fruits and nuts grown here are apples, grapes, bushberries of all kinds, carob, cherimoya, figs, loquats, macadamias, melons of all varieties, peaches, pears, persimmons, plums, pomegranates, sapotes and walnuts. More extensive than this is the variety of vegetables. Among the bunch type are beets, coriander, endive, mustard greens, onions, parsley, radishes, spinach and turnips. Other vegetables include green beans, cauliflower, sweet corn, head lettuce, chili peppers, potatoes, romaine, squash and sweet potatoes. Finally, vying for their own place in the sun but not as commercially important as the others is the group consisting of asparagus, broccoli, chayotes, cherry tomatoes, eggplant, garlic, gourds, green peas and mushrooms.

And there's more. Cattle and calves are fattened and prepared here. Lambs, pigs, turkeys and rabbits are being produced in larger numbers, and the honey business is on the increase. San Diego is home port for the huge white purse-seiner ships that supply the large and well-established tuna industry. All in all, though San Diego's motto is "City in Motion," it might also be said that it is a city of copious cultivation.

BAJA CALIFORNIA DIRECCION (guidance)

Baja California is just across the street, in a manner of speaking, and yet to the United States citizen it's a whole new world. Whether we approve of everything or not is irrelevant; the important thing is that we are guests in a foreign country, presumably pleasure-bound, and as such we are there to make comparisons not problems.

Mexico is not Americanized, despite proximity, and their cities and countryside areas offer much contrast to our way of life. While U.S. freeways may terrorize our foreign visitors, be prepared to have shivers down your back after a drive through busy downtown Tijuana (pronounced Tee-whá-nah). We're just not tuned in to auto and people traffic all doing its own thing as if unaware of possible jeopardy. But that's Tijuana...the Baja California version of Mexico City.

Baja California beaches are quite the opposite. They are vast, sandy stretches of land uncluttered by people or things. Looking at miles of empty coastline you can't help wondering, "Where are the people?"

The back country is similarly fascinating. You can't believe it is so pretty, so unoccupied, and so close to San Diego or Tijuana, until you drive the two-laner highway to Tecate. Even after reaching Tecate, which is unmotivated by tourism, you'll again wonder, "Where are the people?"

Not so in Tijuana. This colorful community is alive, colorful and filled with about 200,000 people, who seem to be all out in the downtown streets. Street vendors, people with and without destinations, move in masses as in highly concentrated areas of New York City...but, oh, so freely. It's across the border with a different set of rules.

The twentieth century has brought a yearly increase in the number of American visitors, with the purpose usually pleasure, an economical Latin holiday. Some make the trip to shop, others come for sports and many just for fun.

Not often can you watch craftsmen at work, but in Tijuana it's possible, while shoppers watch. Glass blowers, wood carvers making furniture or doors, ornamental iron workers, potters and artists abound. Many southern Californians go to Tijuana to buy custom designed Mexican styled creations. Other shoppers are attracted by the duty-free imports of Swiss watches, wearing apparel and perfumes. It makes a nice savings, and U.S. regulations permit you to bring back a total of $100.00 in purchases without taxation.

Sports fans are drawn to Tijuana and nearby Aqua Caliente for the diversity in spectator sports. Caliente's night greyhound racing, or the Jai-Lai games at Tijuana's Fronton Palace, or the corredàs in the Toreo de Tijuana and at the Plaza Monumental Toreo en La Playa (six miles southwest of Tijuana.) Club Campestre, the Tijuana Golf and Country Club, offers a familiar sport in unfamiliar surroundings where you may perhaps get together a foursome composed of Mexicans and Americans.

Some people simply enjoy visiting the "different country" Tijuana restaurants or night life. And as in all cities, certain restaurants stand out for one reason or another. In Tijuana the food is not only Mexican; you can expect a variety of cuisines as the restaurants included here point out. We hope sometime you will visit these mostly-family-owned-and-operated restaurants and that you will also try their fine recipes in your own homes.

Our constantly growing solidarity in small international relationships jointly influences Baja California and San Diego County. This is good…we both have a lot to give.

147

RESTAURANT INDEX
San Diego County

ACAPULCO   131
1733 S. Hill Street
Oceanside   Tel. 729-4454
Dinners from $3.00 up
Lunch & dinner served Mon.-Sat.
    Hours: 11:30 A.M.-11:00 P.M.
Dinner Sunday only
    Hours: 4:00 P.M.-11:00 P.M.
Ample parking
AE, BA, CB, MC credit cards

ANTHONY'S FISH GROTTO   34
Harbor Drive & Ash
San Diego   Tel. 232-5103
886 Prospect
La Jolla   Tel. 454-7135
9530 Murray Drive
La Mesa   Tel. 463-0368
Dinners from $2.00 up
All locations hours:
        11:30 A.M.-8:30 P.M.
Closed Holidays
San Diego Closed Tuesdays
La Jolla and La Mesa closed Mondays
Ample parking
BA credit card
No reservations

ATLANTIS   74
2595 Ingraham Street
San Diego   Tel. 224-2434
Dinners from $4.25 up
Lunch served daily 11:30 A.M.-4:00 P.M.
Dinners served Mon.-Saturday
    Hours: 4:30 P.M.-11:00 P.M.
Dinner Sunday only
    Hours: 4:30 P.M.-10:00 P.M.
Ample parking
AE, BA, DC, MC credit cards
Reservations accepted

BALI HAI   60
2230 Shelter Island Drive
San Diego   Tel. 222-1181
Dinners from $3.25 up

Lunch served Mon.-Fri.
    Hours: 11:30 A.M.-3:30 P.M.
Dinner served Mon.-Thurs.
    Hours: 5:30 P.M.-10:45 P.M.
        Friday
        5:30 P.M.-11:45 P.M.
        Saturday
        5:00 P.M.-12:15 P.M.
        Sunday
        4:00 P.M.-10:30 P.M.
Banquet facilities
Ample parking
AE, BA, CB, DC, MC credit cards
Reservations recommended

BOOM TRENCHARDS   37
2888 Pacific Highway
San Diego   Tel. 291-5555
Dinners from $3.95 up
Lunch served Mon.-Fri. only
    Hours: 11:00 A.M.-3:00 P.M.
Dinner served Mon.-Fri.
    Hours: 5:00 P.M.-11:00 P.M.
        Sat.
        5:00 P.M.-12:00 P.M.
        Sun.
        4:00 P.M.-11:00 P.M.
Ample parking
AE, BA, DC, MC credit cards
Reservations accepted

BRIGANTINE   41
2912 Shelter Island Drive
San Diego   Tel. 224-2871
Dinners from $3.45 up
Lunch served Mon.-Fri.
    Hours: 11:30 A.M.-2:30 P.M.
Dinner served Mon.-Thurs.
    Hours: 6:00 P.M.-11:30 P.M.
Dinner served Fri.-Sat.
    Hours: 6:00 P.M.-12:30 A.M.
Dinner served Sunday only
    Hours: 5:00 P.M.-10:30 P.M.
Ample parking
BA, MC credit cards
Reservations for six or more available
for dinner

148

CAROUSEL 79
Vacation Village
W. Vacation Road & Ingraham
Mission Bay   Tel. 274-4630
Breakfast, lunch & dinner served daily
    Hours: 7:00 A.M.-10:00 P.M.
Ample parking
AE, BA, DC, MC credit cards

CASA DE PICO 30
2754 Calhoun Street
San Diego   Tel. 296-3267
Dinners from $2.25 up
Lunch & dinner served Mon.-Sat.
    Hours: 10:00 A.M.-9:00 P.M.
Lunch & dinner Sunday only
    Hours: 10:00 A.M.-6:00 P.M.
Ample parking
BA, MC credit cards

CHINA LAND CAFE 63
3135 Midway Drive
San Diego   Tel. 223-1255
Dinners from $1.75 up
Dinner served weekdays
    Hours: 4:00 P.M.-3:30 A.M.
Lunch or dinner served Sat. & Sun.
    Hours: 1:00 P.M.-3:30 A.M.
Ample parking
No credit cards
Personal checks ok

CUYAMACA CLUB 44
U.S. National Bank Bldg.
1055 1st Street
San Diego   Tel. 232-6141
Dinners from $5.75 up
Lunch served Mon.-Fri.
    Hours: 12:00 noon-3:00 P.M.
Dinner served Tues.-Sat.
    Hours: 6:00 P.M.-10:00 P.M.
Closed Sundays & Monday nights.
Ample parking
Private club for members and guests
Coat and tie

DEL MAR TURF CLUB 17
Del Mar   Tel. 755-1141
Open July 26th thru Sept. 13th, 1972
Closed on Sundays
Luncheon Buffet from $2.95
    Hours: 12:00-6:30 P.M.
Saturday evening dinner dance
    Hours: 7:00 P.M.-10:00 P.M.
Price of Saturday dinner $8.50 incl. tax
Ample parking
Coat and tie
No credit cards
Reservations necessary

EARL'S SEAFOOD GROTTO 46
Royal Inn at the Wharf
1355 Harbor Drive
San Diego   Tel. 235-6276
Dinners from $4.50 up
Lunch served Mon.-Sat.
    Hours: 11:30 A.M.-2:30 P.M.
Sunday Champagne Brunch
    Hours: 9:30 A.M.-3:00 P.M.
Dinner served Mon.-Sat.
    Hours: 5:00 P.M.-11:00 P.M.
Dinner Sunday only
    Hours: 3:30 P.M.-10:00 P.M.
Banquet facilities
Ample parking
All major credit cards
Reservations accepted

ELARIO'S 81
Summer House Inn
7955 La Jolla Shores Drive
La Jolla   Tel. 459-0261
Dinners from $4.75 up
Lunch served Mon.-Sat.
    Hours: 11:00 A.M.-2:30 P.M.
Sunday Champagne Brunch
    Hours: 10:00 A.M.-2:30 P.M.
Dinner served daily
    Hours: 6:00 P.M.-11:00 P.M.
Ample parking
Coat and tie
All major credit cards
Reservations recommended

FONTAINEBLEAU 85
Westgate Plaza Hotel
1055-1st Street
San Diego   Tel. 232-5011
Dinners from $5.95 up
Lunch served Mon.-Sat.
  Hours: 11:00 A.M.-4:00 P.M.
Dinner served Mon.-Sat.
  Hours: 6:00 P.M.-11:00 P.M.
Closed Sundays
Ample parking
Coat and tie
All major credit cards
Reservations recommended

GOLDEN ROLLIN BELLY 49
225 15th Street
Del Mar   Tel. 755-1414
Dinners from $2.40 up
Brunch served Sunday
  Hours: 12:15 P.M.-2:30 P.M.
Lunch served Mon.-Friday
  Hours: 11:30 A.M.-2:30 P.M.
Dinner served Tues.-Thurs. & Sun.
  Hours: 5:30 P.M.-10:30 P.M.
Dinner served Fri. & Sat.
  Hours: 5:30 P.M.-11:30 P.M.
Ample parking
BA, MC credit cards
No reservations

GRANT GRILL 88
Broadway between 3rd and 4th
San Diego   Tel. 232-3121
Dinners a la carte
Lunch & dinner Mon.-Fri.
  Hours: 11:30 A.M. to Midnight
Dinner only Sat. & Sun.
  Hours: 5:00 P.M. to Midnight
Ample parking
AE, BA, CB, DC, MC credit cards
Reservations accepted

LA COSTA 105
Rancho La Costa   Tel. 729-9111
Dinners from $4.75 up

Main Dining Room and Spa
  Breakfast & Lunch daily
    till 3:00 P.M.
  Dinner daily 7:00 P.M.-10:00 P.M.
Valet parking
Coat daily, Sunday casual
AE, BA, MC credit cards
Reservations necessary

LA FENIERE 67
1466 Garnet Avenue
Pacific Beach   Tel. 272-8540
Dinners from $3.50 up
Dinner served Tues.-Sun.
    Hours: 6:00 P.M.-9:30 P.M.
Closed Mondays
Ample parking
Personal checks—no credit cards
Reservations recommended

LUBACH'S 53
2101 Harbor Drive
San Diego   Tel. 232-5129
Dinners from $3.95 up
Open noon till midnight
Lunch & Dinner Mon.-Sat.
  Hours: 12:00 P.M.-12:00 A.M.
Closed Sundays and holidays
Ample parking
Coat required
BA, MC credit cards
Reservations available

MERCEDES ROOM 55
Bahia Hotel
998 W. Mission Bay Drive
Mission Beach   Tel. 488-0551
Dinners from $3.75 up
Lunch served daily
  Hours: 11:30 A.M.-3:00 P.M.
Dinner served daily
  Hours: 5:00 P.M.-10:00 P.M.
Banquet facilities
Parking lot
All major credit cards
Reservations available

MI BURRO 70

The Royal Inn at the Wharf
1355 Harbor Drive
San Diego   Tel. 232-3861
Dinners from $2.25 up
Lunch & Dinner served Mon.-Fri.
   Hours: 11:00 A.M.-11:00 P.M.
Dinner served Sat. & Sun.
   Hours: 3:00 P.M.-11:00 P.M.
Banquet facilities
Ample parking
All major credit cards

NOTSOM FLOTSOM 90

417 Santa Fe Drive
Encinitas   Tel. 753-0329
Dinner from $2.95 up
Dinner served Mon.-Thurs.
   Hours: 5:00 P.M.-11:00 P.M.
Dinner served Fri. & Sat.
   Hours: 5:00 P.M.-11:30 P.M.
Dinner served Sunday
   Hours: 5:00 P.M.-10:30 P.M.
Ample parking
MC credit card

OLE OLE 92

221 North Highway 101
Solana Beach   Tel. 755-9880
Dinners from $2.45
Lunch & dinner served daily
   Hours: 11:00 A.M.-11:00 P.M.
Ample parking
BA, MC credit cards

PUCCI'S 72

Villa Fontana—Ramada Inn Hotel
2151 So. Hotel Circle
San Diego   Tel. 291-6500
Dinners from $4.95 up
Lunch served Mon.-Fri.
   Hours: 11:30 A.M.-3:30 P.M.
Dinner served Mon.-Fri.
   Hours: 6:00 P.M.-10:30 P.M.
Dinner served Saturday
   Hours: 6:00 P.M.-11:00 P.M.

Banquet facilities
Parking lot
AE, ARCO, BA, CB, CHEVRON,
   DC HUMBLE, MC, RAMADA
   credit cards
Reservations recommended

RANCHO BERNARDO INN 58

17550 Bernardo Oaks Drive
Rancho Bernardo   Tel. 487-1611
Dinners from $4.75 up
Lunch served Mon.-Sat.
   Hours: 11:30 A.M.-2:30 P.M.
Dinner served Mon.-Fri.
   Hours: 6:30 P.M.-10:00 P.M.
Dinner served Saturday
   Hours: 6:30 P.M.-11:00 P.M.
Sunday Brunch
   Hours: 10:30 A.M.-2:30 P.M.
Sunday dinner
   Hours: 5:30-9:00 P.M.
Ample parking
All major credit cards
Reservations necessary

SARRETT HOUSE 96

916 Prospect Street
La Jolla   Tel. 459-3734
Dinners from $3.25 up
Lunch & dinner served Mon.-Thurs.
   Hours: 11:30 A.M.-10:00 P.M.
Lunch & dinner served Fri. & Sat.
   Hours: 11:30 A.M.-11:00 P.M.
Sunday Brunch
   Hours: 10:30 A.M.-5:00 P.M.
Sunday Jam Session
   Hours: 5:00 P.M.-9:00 P.M.
Street parking
BA, MC credit cards
No reservations

SCHNITZELBANK 98

1037 Prospect Street
La Jolla   Tel. 454-5671
Dinners from $2.25 up
Open daily July 1st-Sept. 13th

Otherwise closed Wednesdays
Lunch & dinner served Mon.-Thurs.
  Hours: 11:30 A.M.-9:00 P.M.
Lunch & dinner served Fri. & Sat.
  Hours: 11:30 A.M.-9:30 P.M.
  Brunch & dinner served Sunday
  Hours: 10:30 A.M.-9:00 P.M.
Street parking
BA, MC credit cards

SHANGHAI   138
1017 Prospect Street
La Jolla   Tel. 454-5806
Dinners from $3.25 up
Lunch & dinner served Mon.-Thurs.
  Hours: 11:30 A.M.-10:00 P.M.:
    Fri.-till 11:00 P.M.
Lunch & dinner served Sat. & Sun.
  Hours: 12:00 P.M.-11:00 P.M. Sat.;
    Sun. till 10:00 P.M.
Street parking
BA, MC credit cards
Reservations accepted

STAR OF THE SEA ROOM   140
Anthony's Fish Grotto
Harbor Drive and Ash
San Diego   Tel. 232-7408
Dinners from $4.25 up
Dinner served daily
  Hours: 5:30 P.M.-10:30 P.M.
Closed holidays
Ample parking
Coat and tie
MC credit card
Reservations recommended

TEN DOWNING   100
1250 Sixth Ave.
San Diego   Tel. 235-6566
Dinners from $3.95 up
Lunch served Mon.-Fri.
  Hours: 11:00 A.M.-3:00 P.M.
Dinner served Mon.-Thurs.
  Hours: 5:00 P.M.-10:00 P.M.

Dinner served Fri. & Sat.
  Hours: 5:00 P.M.-11:00 P.M.
Closed Sundays
Ample parking
BA, MC credit cards
Reservations accepted

THE MAD GREEK   32
1250 Prospect Street
La Jolla   Tel. 459-9393
Dinners from $4.50 up
Lunch served daily
  Hours: 11:30 A.M.-2:30 P.M.
Dinner served daily
  Hours: 5:00 P.M.-2:00 A.M.
Street parking
All major credit cards
Reservations accepted

TOM HAM'S LIGHTHOUSE   103
2150 Harbor Island Drive
Harbor Island   Tel. 291-9110
Dinners from $3.50 up
Lunch served Mon.-Fri.
  Hours: 11:30 A.M.-3:30 P.M.
Dinner served Mon.-Thurs.
  Hours: 5:30 P.M.-10:45 P.M.
Dinner served Fri.-Sun.
  Hours: Fri. 5:30 P.M.-11:45 P.M.
    Sat. 5:00 P.M.-12:15 A.M.
    Sun. 4:00 P.M.-10:45 P.M.
Banquet facilities
Ample parking
AE, BA, CB, DC, MC credit cards
Reservations accepted

TORTILLA FLATS   27
887 Camino del Rio South
Mission Valley   Tel. 291-1638
Dinners from $2.65 up
Lunch & dinner served Sun.-Thurs.
  Hours: 11:30 A.M.-10:00 P.M.
Lunch & dinner served Fri. & Sat.
  Hours: 12:00 P.M.-11:30 P.M.
Ample parking
AE, BA, MC credit cards

Baja California Restaurants

BOCCACIO'S 76
Blvd. Aqua Caliente y Gral. Salinas
Tijuana, B.C.
Dinners from $2.25 up
Lunch & dinner served daily,
  closed Wed.
  Hours: 12:00 P.M.-12:00 A.M.
Street parking; parking lots
BA, MC credit cards

CAESAR'S 20
Avenida Revolucion
Tijuana, B.C.
Dinners from $2.95 up
Breakfast, lunch & dinner served daily
  Hours: 8:00 A.M.-11:00 P.M.
Street parking; parking lots
AE, CB, BA, DC, MC, Banco Matico
  credit cards

LA CASITA 51
Tijuana, B.C.
Dinners from $1.75 up
Lunch & dinner served daily
  Hours: 10:00 A.M.-1:00 A.M.
Street parking; parking lots
AE, BA, CD, MC credit cards

LA PERLA 15
Ave. Costera 119
Las Playas de Tijuana, B.C.
Dinners from $2.50 up
Lunch & dinner served daily
Hours: 10:00 A.M.-10:00 P.M.
Ample parking
BA, Banco Matico, MC credit cards

RANCHO LA PUERTA (Resort) 109
Hwy. 2
Tecate, Mexico U.S. Tel. 903-354-1005
American plan hotel $20.00/day up
No credit cards
Reservations necessary

RENO 94
Calle 8a No. 1945
Tijuana, B.C.
Dinners from $3.00 up
Lunch & dinner served daily
  Hours: 11:00 A.M.-3:00 A.M.
Street parking; parking lots
BA, Banco Matico, MC,
  Intra Bank credit cards

SUPER ANTOJITOS 10
Avenida Revolucion 1211
Tijuana, B.C.
Dinners from .95c up
Breakfast, lunch & dinner served daily
  Hours: 24
Street parking; parking lots
No credit cards

VICTORS 24
Aqua Caliente Blvd. y Rio Grijalva
Tijuana, B.C.
Dinners from $2.95 up
Lunch & dinner served daily
  Hours: 12:00 P.M.-11:00 P.M.
Street parking; parking lots
No credit cards

RECIPE INDEX (ALPHABETICAL)

158

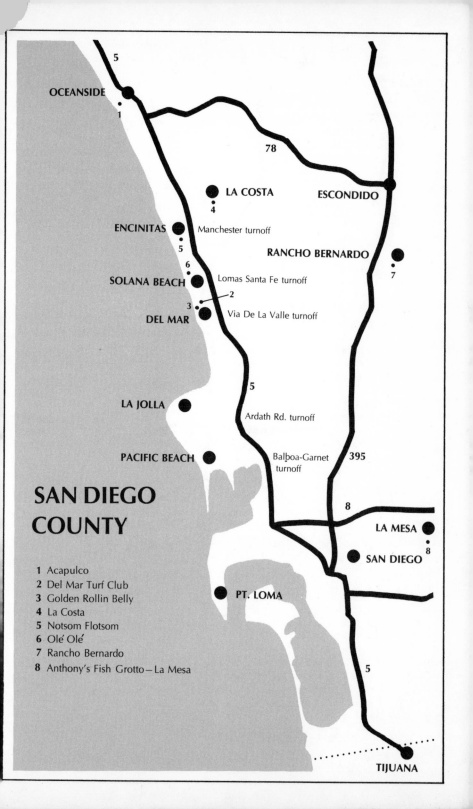

OCEANSIDE
5
1

78
ESCONDIDO

LA COSTA
4

ENCINITAS
Manchester turnoff
5
RANCHO BERNARDO
6
7
Lomas Santa Fe turnoff
SOLANA BEACH
2
3
Via De La Valle turnoff
DEL MAR

5

LA JOLLA
Ardath Rd. turnoff

PACIFIC BEACH
Balboa-Garnet turnoff
395

SAN DIEGO
COUNTY
8
LA MESA
8
SAN DIEGO

1 Acapulco
2 Del Mar Turf Club
3 Golden Rollin Belly
4 La Costa
5 Notsom Flotsom
6 Olé Olé
7 Rancho Bernardo
8 Anthony's Fish Grotto – La Mesa

PT. LOMA

5

TIJUANA

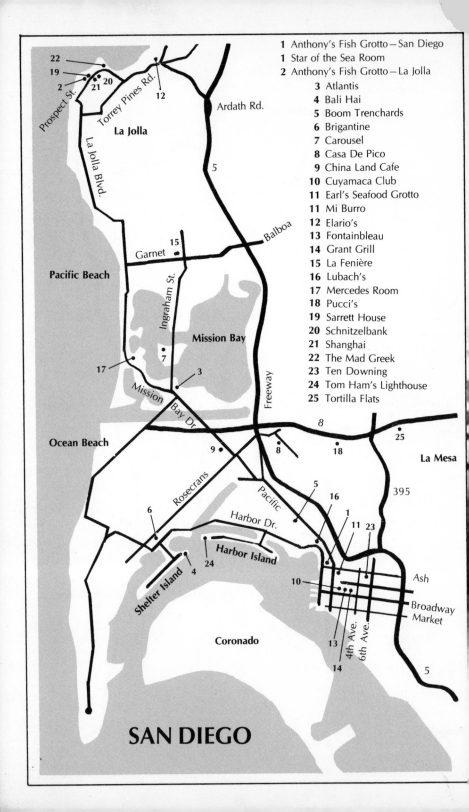

1 Anthony's Fish Grotto—San Diego
1 Star of the Sea Room
2 Anthony's Fish Grotto—La Jolla
3 Atlantis
4 Bali Hai
5 Boom Trenchards
6 Brigantine
7 Carousel
8 Casa De Pico
9 China Land Cafe
10 Cuyamaca Club
11 Earl's Seafood Grotto
11 Mi Burro
12 Elario's
13 Fontainbleau
14 Grant Grill
15 La Fenière
16 Lubach's
17 Mercedes Room
18 Pucci's
19 Sarrett House
20 Schnitzelbank
21 Shanghai
22 The Mad Greek
23 Ten Downing
24 Tom Ham's Lighthouse
25 Tortilla Flats

SAN DIEGO